I0234543

THE KEY

SETHIAN GNOSTICISM IN
THE POSTMODERN WORLD

RUNE ØDEGAARD

KRYSTIANIA

Published 2011 by Krystiania

© Rune Ødegaard 2011

Cover: Rune Ødegaard & Joachim Svela

ISBN 978-82-998243-7-8

CONTENTS

4

"It is not the time of the creation in itself that disturbs us, nor is it the so-called fall, or the time when mankind wandered the world between light and darkness.
What disturbs us is what we suspect transpired in the time before time".

Magister Amarantus
Sodalitas Sanctum Seth

This book is dedicated to the pilgrims of Light, who carry the sacred Mysteries of God and Man through the decades of light and darkness, until the end of the world.

About this book

The intention of this book is to convey a basic understanding of Sethian Gnosticism from a participatory point of view via the reading of its myths. This book is written from an inside perspective. It does not seek to be considered an academic work but to give a balanced presentation of an often misunderstood tradition.

The book will shed some light on this path from a contemporary perspective, from the view of a practising carrier of this tradition, and show how Sethian use of Gnostic stories can be a key to freedom and peace. By doing this the reader might gain an understanding of the position of Man, his mental and spiritual compositions, and his life in the world from the view of this tradition.

I do not wish to promote a Gnostic religion, but to give an interpretational key for those who are considering exploring this tradition.

This book is not an introduction to Gnosticism, as several good introductory books have already been written. Amongst these are Elaine Pagels's *The Gnostic Gospels*, and Stephan Hoeller's *Gnosticism in a New Millennium*.

This book is for those who already have a basic understanding of the topic at hand and is a guide for those who are seeking to understand the special character of modern Sethian Gnosticism.

I hope this work will be beneficial and inspirational for those seeking to explore the greatest mystery that exists, namely that of Man.

ACKNOWLEDGMENTS

I wish to thank everyone who has helped me with this book, and especially:

Kjersti, my wife, for good counsel on all my writings.

David and Howard, dear friends in the Gnostic Society, who invested hour upon hour translating and proof reading this book from Norwegian into English.

Joachim, my friend and partner in several esoteric adventures.

INTRODUCTION

From the nineteenth century until the present day, many books on Gnosticism have been written. Many of these books present stories and topics that often seem to be in direct contradiction with each other and can easily confuse readers. This misunderstanding is based upon the fact that they describe many different systems of thought where redemption is based on experience, rather than faith. Therefore, by way of introduction, we need to establish a distinction between Gnosis-based systems and Gnosticism in the strict sense of the term.

While Gnosis-based teachings may refer to various experience-based ways to a religious goal, a Gnostic system of thought must include a variation of the main elements of the Gnostic myth. Some of these elements will be presented in this book.

However, Gnosticism as a collective term does have similarities in both myths and theology which gives it a distinctive character. It would therefore be just as misleading to talk about Reiki Gnosticism as a Buddhist Pentecostal movement.

The author of this book will not judge true prophets from false ones, but has included a reading list at the end of this book, for those who want to read material similar to what is presented here.

To the knowledge of the author, no previous books contain an inside perspective on the Gnostic school of Sethianism, also known as Classical Gnosticism. Even less has been published that contain its modern reading and use of traditional mythological stories and ritual materials.

This book is, therefore such a curious thing as an introduction to Gnostic Sethian interpretational methods, as taught in the Sethian mystery school of *Sodalitas Sanctum Seth*.

This book will be the first book of a trilogy.

This first book provides an introduction to Sethianism and how to use Sethian texts as redemption-triggers.

The second book, *The Gate*, will be a collection of modern Sethian texts with introductory commentaries. These will be texts from the school of *Sodalitas Sanctum Seth*.

The third book will consist of descriptions of practices and ceremonies from the Sethian society, with comments from the author.

Taken together, these books provide a fundamental and broad understanding of the nature of modern Sethianism as an independent tradition and part of the spiritual family of Gnosticism.

Gnosticism differs from many other spiritual paths, as it is based on direct personal experience rather than faith. Therefore it goes without saying that even this book cannot convey Gnosis but it will point the reader to a path leading to the possibility of discovering it him or herself.

This book might thus be a key for those who are seeking, for those who are at a certain point in life, where they are ready to find.

The book is therefore not only an introduction into the Sethian tradition, but also a mystery in itself. If the reader absorbs the Gnostic story, here called *The Book of Eleleth*, or even just reads it carefully, Gnostic processes may be initiated in the depths of the reader's mind.

So please remember that whenever you are approaching material of this nature, that while you are reading, the book is also reading you.

Rune Ødegaard
Oslo, Norway
Epiphany 2009

FAITH AND GNOSIS:
TWO TYPES OF RELIGION, AND A
PATHLESS PATH

Since the creation of written language, and probably even earlier, people have sought the meaning, the understanding and the purpose of humanity's existence. Countless teachers, prophets, and holy men and women have pointed in different directions to show us where we should go, how we should live, and how we should die. They have gathered, organized, and interpreted the teachings, signs and phenomena. They have built religious organizations to provide a greater common understanding of the purpose of human life. The religions of the world have systematized and institutionalized the teachings of the founders; and adapted them to meet their context: their people, culture and society.

Throughout this history a pattern has repeated itself. There are enthusiasts who have had a certain personal experience of something different, curious and spiritual. They then further interpret this experience as sacred, or even as entering the presence of God. These experiences often occur within the framework of an already existing religious or spiritual tradition, thereby leading to some form of renewal or reformation. Buddha and Rudolf Steiner can be taken as examples of two such individuals who created something new based on something existing, respectively Hindu and Christian mythology. Both had experiences that renewed existing doctrine and laid the foundations for a new spiritual path. This can act as a correction or an antithesis to the status quo.

These enthusiasts then receive students who have not had any direct experiences of their own, but who have confidence in the experience of the founder. The audience is thus not expected to have equal illuminations, but instead get to stand in the position of receivers, in contrast to the one who started the movement. Since they have no direct experiences themselves, and do not have direct personal experience with its origin, they relate themselves, in most cases dogmatically, to the doctrine which has been supplied by the teacher.

In this way the organization solidifies the dogmas and develops the structures, until a new enthusiast has an illuminating experience.

The organization must then decide whether the experience is in line with their understanding of the original teachings. If not, they would probably reject it, and declare it as heretical revelations, and banish them from their society.

It requires a structured hierarchical system to run an organization that distributes laws, meaning, and content; to be able to enforce teachings within this framework and to have influence on society at large.

In today's western post-modern society the major religious organizations are standing at a crossroads. Social homogeneity and traditional communities are splitting up, and the fate of the great ideologies has shown that universalism cannot stand the test of time.

Individualism, independence and personal involvement in constructing knowledge are replacing old religious thinking, dependence and belief. Ours is a society where sincere seekers are in danger of seeking out the extremes. This may lead to forms of strict sectarian involvement where mankind drowns doubt and pluralism of meaning together with the ownership of individual understanding and the value of our own experiences. In these traditions the dogmas, rules and Holy Scriptures form a cognitive cage which suffocates life and personal understanding, until the cage is internalized as a self-sustaining part of the personality.

On the other hand, we have people who let go of all previous beliefs and experiences of truth and choose a path purely based on feelings and intuition.

Without any form of map or compass, they leave for a spiritual fragmented supermarket; moving from shop to shop, from teaching to teaching, course after course, in search of adventures to incite, satisfy, and arouse their spiritual life.

Such people measure the value of each of the different spiritual paths by its ability to trigger stimulating feelings, which are interpreted as direct contact with gods and angels. This road leads its pilgrims to an experience-addiction, where experiences of all-otherness, is often more important than the significance of them. In this case, the teacher's charisma may be far more important than knowledge and facts.

The picture being drawn here is obviously a rough description of personality types. A more moderate characterization would be to see them as points on a continuum where at one end the ultra-dogmatic are situated and at the other end are the pluralistic and unstructured new agers.

These two human types will be discussed further in the book, where the first is described as *Abelian* (by Abel, Adam's second son) and the other *Cainite* (by Cain, Adam's first son). According to Gnostic tradition, both of these approaches are misleading. The need to understand the meaning of the Mystery of existence, of Man and God cannot be acquired through dogmatic subordination or trust in the volatile temper of the ever changing senses.

This book points to a path, which is not a path, but rather a path between the paths. It is a story told at the strike of the thirteenth hour on the mystical dial of the wise; from a mental position between truth and falsehood, reality and dream, in a spiritual place that unites all things in a point without a centre.

This tradition is based on Biblical stories of creation, the nature of God, how man came to live on earth, and how we may recapture what humanity lost. The tradition, to which this book refers, has a systematic enquiring approach to redemption. It thus relies on our own understanding and our own experiences to grasp it.

This is the path called Gnosticism; Sethian Gnosticism.

GNOSIS, SETHIANISM AND CHARAXIO

Gnosticism as the word suggests is knowledge or experience-based knowledge. This raises a natural question: What is it that the Gnostics know?

The answer to this is simple yet complicated and it relates to the true relationship between God, Man and nature. It is who we are, where we came from, and where we are going. The answer to these questions is what this book and many esoteric schools and orders refer to as the Mystery.

The Mystery is a realization that by itself brings about a change in the being of the one who has had this special experience. There are other mysteries or secrets; but none surpasses the significance of the understanding brought forth by this singular phenomenon.

Living in Gnosis, to live according to and in unity with this Mystery, might be compared to living according to a highly integrated philosophy. But it is better to compare it to the experience of looking at a 3D image that first just looks like dots and colours, but is designed so that if one stares into it, and beyond it, an underlying image emerges from the seemingly meaningless patterns.

Gnosticism as a concept is a very imprecise term, which only says something about the approach. It's like putting Catholicism, Mormonism and the Bahaí-religion together with all other faith-based religions, and calling them *Pistisism* (*pistis* = faith), since all are faith-based religions. The division of Pistisism and Gnosticism has a value in the sense that it points out the precise approach in the two perspectives. The term Pistisism will therefore be used further in this book, since from a Gnostic perspective; there is no need to distinguish between the faith-based belief systems.

SETHIANISM

Gnosticism, as described in this book, is Sethian Gnosticism or Sethianism. Sethianism is named after Adam's third son Seth, and it had its golden age from about 300BC, to 300AD. Sethianism was one of the many so-called Gnostic schools that were as diverse in their organizations and movements as Pistisism is today.

This Gnostic path is among the oldest of the organized Gnostic schools that had a basic systematic theology, with common sacraments and initiated members.

During the first period of about 600 years, the tradition probably had three major reforms, as reflected in the texts that were found buried at Nag Hammadi in Egypt in 1945.

This text collection, which is the most important discovery of Gnostic literature, was probably buried as these writings were forbidden by canonical Christianity. It was found by a shepherd who initiated the challenging journey of these scriptures, before most of them were handed over to scientists who translated and published them.

The three Sethian periods, or reforms, were a Jewish period, a Christian period and a Platonic period. In all these reforms, the Gnosis from earlier periods was clothed with new garments. This means that the forms were changed while the core remained untouched.

It is the Judeo-Christian version of the Mysteries that gives form to the descriptions given in this book, as it may seem to be the Judeo-Christian form which became the foundation for most of the later branches of the Gnostic family tree.

Charaxio

In the early Sethian texts, it is said that Seth hid his secrets on the top of a mountain. This mountain is referred to as Mount Charaxio.

This is probably not a mountain with a physical location in the world, but another place in another dimension, a state of mind, of dream, or wakeful sleep. The description of this central mountain has associated the Sethians with people living in the mountains.

The doctrine that was hidden on Charaxio is like a pattern of archetypal dream images, which might be compared to an archetypal 'radio station'. Sethians tap into this channel for inspiration.

In the *Sodalitas Sanctum Seth* the *Charaxio* is also a book. This book consists of three parts. The first part is the old Sethian texts, and consists currently of *The Apocryphon of John*, *The Book of the Great Invisible Spirit* (also known as *The Gospel of the Egyptians*), *The Hypostasis of the Archons*, *The Thought of Norea*, *The Naassene*

Psalm, The Three Steles of Seth, Trimorphic Protennoia, The Apocalypse of Adam, Allogenes, The book of Allogenes, Melchizedek, Marsanes, Zostrianos, The Gospel of Thomas and *The Gospel of Judas*.

The Gospel of Thomas and *The Naassean Psalm* are not described as Sethian texts, since the Sethian mythology is not directly connected to these books. They are, however, still used within the modern manifestation of the tradition.

The second section consists of explanations, interpretations, narratives, and letters, of which *The Book of Eleleth* is published in this book, while the other texts are currently reserved for the initiates of *Sodalitas Sanctum Seth*. More of these will be included in the next book of this trilogy. This second part of the Charaxio is an expression of the vitality of the tradition. It requires that the Sethians are able to express Gnosis in an ever original way, as language creates the reality of which we all are part.

The third part consists of rituals, ceremonies, instructions for practice and Gnostic sacraments.

Charaxio is not a canon, as a canon is a fixed form, coagulated by history and culture. The Gnostics' journey is to each their own and cannot be explained in simple dogma; Life itself is our canon. Therefore, *Charaxio* should more rightly be called a book of inspiration, or a compass for the Gnostic journey.

CONTROVERSIAL
INTERPRETATIONS

In this chapter we will attempt to resolve some of the most common misunderstandings relating to the classic Gnostic stories. Many of these stem from the time when the Christian church fathers wrote their polemical works against the Gnostic communities. The spirit of these works, such as Irenaeus's *Against Heresies*, has also taken new and modern forms in discussions that the author has had with Pistisists.

The problem with defending Gnosticism with words is that Gnosis does not denote a linear or logical experience. It is only the tip of the iceberg that is seen above the water that can be described and referred to. The rest of the iceberg, which is the main part of the mountain, is hidden in systems of experience, interpretation, and life experience. Gnosticism is a mental leap into the unimaginable and unknown. It requires a drastic *eureka* moment that turns the mind to a full understanding of the mountain's shape.

The reader will be presented with an opportunity to glimpse what is beneath the surface. To prepare the reader for the plunge, we will address some commonly occurring mental obstacles; namely: the idea of Gnosticism constituting an united body, the criticisms of elitism, dualism and Satanism, and some ideas concerning the alleged negative Gnostic attitude towards the body and sexuality.

GNOSTICISM AS AN UNITED BODY

To understand Gnosticism, it would be wise to look at it from different angles and then connect each text to its source tradition within the Gnostic family. An important note in relation to these texts is that Gnosticism as such, does not have a 'Canon' or 'Bible', nor did the early Christians prior to ca 400AD. One of the first attempts at compiling a canon was made by Marcion of Sinope. He wanted to base the New Testament on the Gospel of Luke and a selection of Paul's letters. The response to his efforts can be found in the manuscript known as the Easter letter of Athanasius from the year 367AD. This letter describes the books that would become The New Testament, which the Roman Emperor Constantine supported and his descendants established as the only orthodox (i.e. legal) form of Christian Religion.

The Gnostics had little, if any, desire to create a canon, as a canon denotes a collection of texts presenting officially approved versions of encounters with the Holy. For the Sethians, books are only the outer shape or mask of this Mystery. Ultimately, one might also question whether it is even possible to communicate the Mystery in a complete form via the written word.

What holds the Sethian tradition together is a story. The Gnostic narrative has elements that are part of its template, but have no fixed form. It can be told in any language or mythical form. Sethianism used the Old Testament, New Testament and Platonism but could just as easily use Egyptian mythology or the cult of Mithras to give shape to the Gnosis. The Mystery is independent of divine names and mythologies. It is a set of tools to present it within any given cultural framework.

In our time, we might say that the novelist Philip K. Dick and the movie *The Matrix* represent modern forms of the same Gnostic story. The entertainment industry does not usually teach

Gnosticism, but might unintentionally or intentionally serve as keys and road signs for those who are affected by them, or so that those who have ears may hear…

ELITISM

Classical Gnosticism was a closed initiatory society, which focused on a specific realization or experience, instead of faith or beliefs. Through history this fact has led people to criticize it for being elitist and secretive. There are two elements in this; its closed character and the focus on the experience.

In the period from 300BC to 300AD, which is called Hellenism, the mystery schools were a natural part of life in the region where Christianity was born. Christianity originally also presented itself as such a society, but had an unusual rule. Membership was exclusive in the sense that it excluded membership in any other religious or spiritual community. This was an ill omen heralding the dominant and intolerant role that Christianity would take in the future.

The transition into Christian dominance began when the Emperor Constantine gave the Roman Catholic religion the right to practise in the Roman Empire. Consummation of this occurred when his descendant Theodosius in 392AD gave the Roman Catholic Church a religious monopoly. Further, those who continued to follow other religious orientations would be put to death if they were discovered.

Today Sethians are more open than during the Hellenistic period. The Sethian narrative in its basic form can be found in *The Apocryphon of John*. It is this myth which is used as background for Gnostic sacramental practices that support individual development and redemption. It is by living the myth that one understands its functional effect on the mind and the soul.

To be able to receive anything from a Gnostic school, you have to have had some kind of Gnostic experience, or be in search of the Mystery. Exactly what this means is difficult to explain, as there may be several signs indicating that such a process is in progress. It might begin as an existential suspicion that something fundamental is wrong with the composition of the world.

Through a discussion with someone initiated, someone who has received the Mystery, it is possible to confirm whether one's experience is of a Gnostic character or not. As indicated above, it does not have to be some great spiritual experience; it might be that he or she has found a fragile point in the fabric of the universe through art or philosophy.

The criteria of personal effort to open the inner door should not suggest elitism. It is rather a question of whether you will take responsibility for your own spirituality, rather than outsourcing it to someone else.

The criteria of responsible collection of experience and critical thinking should not frighten or disturb modern men or women. Those who condemn people for their spiritual and existential experiences and their yearning for freedom have rather disturbing priorities. They favour a more passive role as followers, and call the first elitists, to justify their taking the softer option.

DUALISM

To understand the criticism of dualism (i.e. that reality is composed of two incompatible forces: e.g. good and evil or spirit and matter), one must dive into the mythological material. At this point the discussion will only serve as an introduction to the issues surrounding the Sethian understanding of God. This is a mystery; some parts can be explained, and some are within the experience based part of the tradition.

The criticism is not that difficult to explain as it is mainly based on misunderstandings of the Gnostic teachings when approached from a Pistisist point of view.

In simple words, one might say that there is an absolute reality and its reflected abortion. The absolute reality is a non-material creation, or emanation, which exists in a state of perfect harmony. At this level of existence, everyone takes part in each other's being, even to the extent of the Great Invisible Spirit which is the Monad or God. This place, which is not a place, is called *Pleroma* or the Fullness.

This Fullness is mirrored through a junction where everything above is casting a distorted shadow into the empty void. It is the creation of the ego in a world where everything is a form of meditative reality.

This junction between the above and below is the generation of the entities that in the Gnostic tradition are known as *Yaldabout*, the creator of the universe, and *Nebroel*, the rebel and opposer.

The world is a coagulated material manifestation of their interaction with each other.

This means that the world is neither good nor evil; it is only a forfeited dimension of being, where there is no causal connection between kindness and living a long and good life, between how one chooses to live and a just reward. There is further no connection between the human love of the creator god and the creator's love for us.

The Sciences can give us principles of what to eat, and suggest activities that are good for our health, to improve our possibilities of a good and long life. But nothing can insure us against accidental illness, death or unforeseen poverty. In these matters, there is nothing that indicates that the creator protects those who are faithful to him.

Yaldabout and Nebroel represent the ego's constant battle against itself, the tensions in the creation, and their being are like two sides of same coin. Yaldabout makes rules for right behaviour, promises for eternal reward and punishment in the afterlife, while his counterpart Nebroel is the outlaw who disregards the rules, encourages worldly pleasures and a quest for materialistic fulfilment.

Together they represent a mental prison; they occupy the human mind so that one cannot raise one's eyes from the polar tensions of the creation.

Sethianism is thus closer to monism, the view that all processes and phenomena in the world are attributable to one singular principle. The only thing that really exists is the Pleroma.

Yaldabout and Nebroel are the guardians of the dream (or nightmare) that humans experience as the worldly life. Through the recognition and rectification of this dual nature, one can live in the world without being of the world. One will then not cling to false hopes and fears of what might seem to be fate. Rather one will compose one's own life and consider one's relationship to oneself, one's fellow beings, and the world.

All that is required is that you wake up from the mythical and cultural dream.

Satanism

Many Gnostic texts do distinguish between Yaldabout and Nebroel, or God and Satan. Yaldabout appears with the qualities of both. He rewards and punishes in a way that according to modern civilized standards would be labelled unfair and often unnecessarily cruel.

Classical Gnosticism does not have a very positive evaluation of the creator of this world, and believes that he is not the true God, but a demiurge (i.e. a craftsman or demi-creator). He is a craftsman who acts as a god by his own rules. These rules do not seem to be suitable for his creation, as he constantly has to punish, torture and kill his subjects in order to make them conform to his rule, even those who love him and try to follow his ways.

A good example of the craftman's shifting and unpredictable moods is the story of Korah in Numbers 16:21-46. In this tale God draws Korah, his family and all his relatives alive down to Hell, because they wanted to serve God, as Aaron and Moses did. On top of that, God tells the survivors to collect the embers of the hellfire, and make metal plates to dress his altar, since the embers had been sanctified by his touch ...

Gnostics do rather look in favor upon Korah, for his desire to have a more active and intimate relationship with God; but alas, he was unlucky to meet the moody Creator God who decides to massacre him together with his whole family.

Yaldabout, the creator, has his own heroes in these stories. These are often belligerent leaders of the people, such as for example, David, Aaron and Joshua. Gnostics do not consider these shining war heroes to be heroes at all, some are even seen as antagonists to Gnosis.

From a Sethian point of view, the antagonists of the Bible are divided into two categories. They may belong to Nebroel who makes people break away from Yaldabout's laws, but in so doing further engages them in the dualistic perspective, on the side of the Master of materialism and darkness.

The other type of biblical antagonist comes from the Pleroma to contribute to the liberation of Man from the life of shades of black and white and the chains of blinding sleep and conformity. Examples of these are the Snake of the Garden of Eden, Seth and Judas.

It is important to understand that this may be understood psychologically as well as religiously. It must in no way be regarded as dogma but rather as images of a reality that exist side by side in mythology and in our everyday lives. The only individual that can distinguish between the agents of Yaldabout, Nebroel, and the Pleroma is the individual who has Gnosis. This is the only true measure of distinction that can be used on secular experience and human relations, as well as on divine revelations. For Yaldabout and his supporters the result would be the same, whether a rule is broken out of disrespect for the law (Nebroel), or in order to break the chains that keep the human mind trapped in the cognitive prison (Pleroma).

Sethian stories tell how the serpent in the Garden of Eden helped to liberate man from his drugged state of captivity in a mentally passive and meaningless vacuum.

Yaldabout wants man to strive to uphold impossible rules, but it is impossible to fit Man into such a psychological cage. Doing so might even cause anxiety and mental disorders. Quite a few people who suffer from psychosis believe that God will punish them if they do not maintain certain patterns of behaviour. Yaldabout keeps his followers in check by threatening with a severe penalty and by offering the possibility of reconciliation

27

through taking on additional duties or carrying greater burdens of self-inadequacy.

It is important for these opposing forces that the struggle between good and evil persists. Without one, the other could not exist and human souls that are caught in this paradigm would, as in Plato's allegory of the cave, turn around and see reality and the goodness of a life in freedom.

So, to conclude the issue of Satanism, it is unreasonable to call a Gnostic who does not believe in Satan's independent existence, and who does not worship Satan, a Satanist. But if a Satanist is to be defined as one who does not believe that the world's creator is The Supreme God, as defined by traditional Christian orthodoxy, then all Gnostics are truly Satanists.

The body

Reading the Sethian texts, and especially *The Secret Book of John*, it might seem as if the body is generally described as an unconditioned evil, which is binding, confusing and destructive to the Gnostic redemption process. Such a reading of the text is too narrow. Although the body has no purpose in itself, it plays an important part when we are in the world.

Understanding the body's function is linked to the Sethian story of the body as a creation of the Rulers (i.e. the various artisans who are subject to the Demiurge).

The body is not evil, but it constitutes a challenge. It constantly needs attention and care. It gives rise to pleasure and pain, leading perception away from the spiritual into a state of chronic everyday consciousness and unawareness. It is a challenge as it is closely connected to our spirit nature, through the soul. This means that the body must work, at the very least, at a minimum level so that one can use it as a spiritual processing tool.

Old age is regarded, by some Sethians, as useful in this case in that it can facilitate the actualization of the Mystery. In old age one may realize that one is not the body, as much of its vitality and beauty will have faded, and with them the attachment to it. The only thing left that can stand in the way is fear of death or serious illness which can rob one of one's sanity.

The body was made according to divine sketches even though bad materials were used in its creation. This turns the body into a map or a set of riddles that once understood and known, may provide important keys to understanding and redemption. For where there is a lock, there is also a key.

SEXUALITY

There are many perspectives on sexuality in the Gnostic tradition, just as in the Pistic religions. These perspectives illuminate both disruptive and fulfilling perspectives as indicated in the tale of Cain, Abel and Seth's conception, in *The Secret Book of John*. In the Sethian story, only Seth is conceived by Adam and Eve. Cain is the child of Eve and Nebroel and Abel is the child of Eve and Yaldabout.

Thus it should be obvious that there is a potential danger associated with sex. This means that it should be treated with thoughtfulness and awareness, as it is intimately related to self-actualization in the body, well-being, and the feeling of belonging in the world, not to mention the potential manifestation of a child.

In Sethianism sex is beneficial if the parties involved recognize the divinity in each other, so they may unite as do the pairs in the Pleroma. Sexual union is thus not just a product of physical pleasure, of violence or perversion, but of seeking an experience of union, wholeness and bliss, which also characterizes parts of the redemption process.

Sethianism does not, however, condemn sexual relations for the sake of pure lust or sex with individuals regardless of dedication. But in dealing with sexuality in this way, one must be vigilant, so that it does not create emotional problems and relational difficulties, which contribute to an inappropriate bonding to creation.

The turning of the Gnostic Wheel

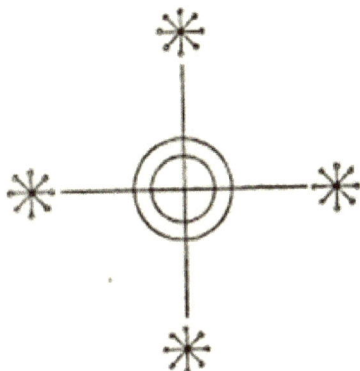

The first turning: The Beginning

From about 300 BC until around 300 AD, Gnostic masters developed different stories. These stories, though numerous and often very different, convey the same knowledge and Mystery. The similarity in these early stories is that Humanity was created holy, infinite and divine. Humanity or "Man" was created as a spiritual being, which through divine tragedy became trapped in material form and thus in worldly darkness.

The stories say that it is not Satan or some simplistic force of pure evil that keeps humanity trapped. Rather it is the world's creator, pretending to be man's divine Father, that has enslaved humanity into ignorance and death.

Early traditions, as described in several of the Nag Hammadi texts, say that by acknowledging his origins Man can influence his own salvation.

Sethianism has a story about how the tradition came to be. It is described in *The Book of the Great Invisible Spirit*, also called the *Gospel of the Egyptians*. This text says the following about the historical seed of Seth:

> "The great Seth came and planted his seed in the Aeons down here and its number is the number of Sodom. Some say that Sodom is the pasture of the Great Seth, which is Gomorrah. Others say that the Great Seth took his crop from Gomorrah and planted it somewhere else, which he called Sodom [...] This is the source of the kin of the eternal life, which belongs to them that have gained knowledge about where they came from. This is the Great Immovable Race."

Seth and his spiritual children, called Sethians, constitute a spiritual race. This race or spiritual lineage has moved throughout time and history. This lineage has coiled through the shades of history, embodied by sages and initiators. They serve to ensure that men and women constantly have access to the redemptive mystery, and further they leave stories and myths for subsequent generations to read and study.

The myth states that Seth knew the ruling powers were trying to destroy the initiates and the teachings.

For the protection of his seed, and their future work, Guardian Angels were set over it to protect it, as stated in *The Book of the Great Invisible Spirit*:

> "Seth asked for guardians of his seed [...] They were followed by the great Aerosiel and the great Selmechel. They were sent to protect the Immovable Seed, its people and its fruits."

In this sense the Sethian bloodline is a line of knowledge and a Mystery that has survived history regardless of any specific name and specific practices. One can find traces of an unbroken Sethian lineage, or fragments of an experience in practice, throughout the history of the secret societies of Europe.

This is supported by the somewhat romantic notion that the Gnostic tradition could not be stamped out by the establishment of a uniform, orthodox Christianity in the 4th and 5th centuries. The Sethian vessel entered Valentinianism, which for a time coexisted with nascent Catholicism.

Valentinianism is a term which was probably coined by the early Church fathers in order to label a tradition viewed as deviant and therefore heretical, and it refers to a movement founded by Valentinus (ca 100-160), who possibly came from Egypt. He was one of the first systematic theologians, and his project was to reconcile the Classical Gnostic tradition with the tradition that by the fourth century would become the Catholic Church.

Consequently, Valentinianism was a mixture of Catholic and initiatory Gnostic Christianity. It was Catholic in the sense that it probably used Baptism and Confirmation as the basis and preparation for the traditional Gnostic teachings.

At this time the church was initiatory in its form, and Valentinians viewed the sacraments as steps in a process leading to Gnosis. By being an initiatory system all the steps that aspirants took in the process were probably evaluated and discussed between the initiated and the initiator.

Because of this reconciliation the Valentinians were using Catholic sacramental forms as vehicles for the Spirit of the Gnostic Mystery. The sacraments of Baptism and Confirmation were probably proto-Christian, as described in the *Didaché*. The inner school consisted of the Valentinian sacraments of Redemption and Bridal Chamber as described in the *Gospel of Philip*.

Men and women had equal rights to speak and to be ordained priests. As a church community the Valentinian internal organization probably consisted of small congregations, to protect the intimate character of the Mystery.

A distinctive feature of the Valentinian tradition was that they replaced the Sethian sombre version of the demiurge by Plato's theory about an ignorant but well-intentioned craftsman, as described in *Timaeus*.

Valentinians used Platonism, Sethianism and many of the texts that later became the New Testament, but used their own interpretive keys. In addition they had several texts, which they wrote, and continued to write on an ongoing basis. Among these, the best known texts are *The Gospel of Truth* and *The Gospel of Philip*.

Thus Sethianism and Valentinianism constitute two of the most important traditions of early Gnosticism. Sethianism was a mystery school and an order, and had its own magical system, whereas Valentininanism was the union of Gnosticism and Pistisism.

Both of these forms of teaching the Mystery disappeared after Catholicism became the only legal religion in the Roman Empire. The last official account, from the Catholic church, of Sethian and Valentinian operative schools dates from the seventh century.

Out of sight, but not out of mind.

The second turning: The Recovery

In the Middle Ages the Manicheans, the Cathars and partly
also the Guild system became carriers of the Gnostic seeds.
Manichaeism was founded by Mani (210-276), who probably
received his training in a small and closed Gnostic community.
When he left this tradition, he took with him its core and
developped a religion that spread all over the known world,
and can thus be called a historical world religion. This is also
the only world religion that has died out. This happened as a
result of where the Manicheans lived, which was also the main
seat of Islam, and unlike Manichaeism, Islam did not have a
commandment of pacifism in its missionary work. It was a
different story in Asia where Manicheans held their ground until
the 1500s.

Manichaeism has many similarities with the French
interpretation of Christianity espoused by the Cathars in the
southern part of France. It is conceivable that there was an
overlap and continuation of the Gnostic teachings from the
Manicheans to the Cathars. Many similarities can be seen
between their Gnostic narratives.

The Cathar Church was destroyed by a home mission crusade
that killed clergy and faithful by the thousands, and thus put an
end to this impulse from the mid-13th century and up to 1330.

After that, parts of the tradition might have survived through
the Guild system in Scotland (cf. Ramsay's well known Masonic
lesson, *Oration*), and in family traditions.

Elements from these small units were woven into the dawning
initiatory orders of the Renaissance and Enlightenment eras, as
described, for example, in the Rosicrucian manifestoes of the
early 17th century.

In this tradition Seth is described as *Helias Artista*. This branch is described further by Joachim Svela in his book of the same name.

From the Renaissance onwards, the dormant Sethian tradition was resurfacing. From the beginning of the 1600s until this present day several esoteric organizations are consciously and unconsciously carrying bits and pieces of the Gnostic legacy.

Elements from Valentinian tradition were taken into high degree systems of Freemasonry through Martinez de Pasqually's *Élus Cohen*. A system that still exists within the Martinist order *Ordre Reaux Croix*, as well as in some other orders. Elements from Manichaeism moved into the Egyptian Masonic traditions.

In the 1800s the Gnostic Church tradition re-emerged in France, through Jules Doinel (1842-1903), when he proclaimed a new Gnostic era in 1890. This led to the founding of the *Église Gnostique*.

This church had its own sacraments and its own clergy that based its work on the sources they had access to at that time. Those who were attracted to this church were mainly those who were already members of esoteric orders associated with the Gnostic tradition.

As the Gnostic tradition manifested itself in forms similar to its origin, it inspired apostolically ordained bishops, which in turn led to the Gnostic churches being re-infused with the apostolic succession; including the lineages of Peter, Andrew and Thomas. The liturgical shape of these churches was Catholic in their symbolic language, but with a Gnostic content. The reason for this is probably that their founders' backgrounds were mainly from the Catholic Church. This led many of these churches to become associated with Valentinus, who had had a similar project hundreds of years earlier.

The hallmark of most of the new Gnostic church traditions is that they do not differentiate between the various Gnostic movements. Rather it is as but patches put together from all various Gnostic sources creating Pan-Gnostic structures. The Pan-Gnostic structure has many internal contradictions in relation to its teachings and practices. This might give room for free thinking, with great focus on the sacramental community, or lead to confusion.

Since the finding of the first Gnostic texts in the 1700s, up to more recent discoveries, such as The Nag Hammadi finding in 1945, these texts have served to promote the general awareness that the Gnostic tradition is a tradition in itself. Just as the Kabbalah and Hermeticism are independent traditions, so was also Gnosticism and this was an important aid to the rising Gnostic Churches.
Thanks to the discoveries at Nag Hammadi we have been given even greater insight into the differences and mutability of the Early Gnostic founders, their texts, orders and churches.

The second shift of the Gnostic wheel ends with the aftermath of World War II and the end of the Cold War. During this period, a great number of churches were established or re-established. These bodies explored a variety of Gnostic, Hermetic, Kabbalistic, and other materials. Among the most typical examples of such organizations are *Ecclesia Gnostica* and *Ecclesia Gnostica Apostolica*. Many Gnostic Churches would follow in the twentieth century which has been marked by increased prosperity and development in the West.

The period ends with greater openness in society, increased social equality, expanding communication and technology, and the challenging of old authoritarian institutions and values; it ended in postmodernism.

This gave rise to a new reformation within the Gnostic organizations, an *Ad-fontes*-reformation which led to *Restorational Gnosticism*, with its organizations and churches focussing on developing the different Gnostic schools on the foundations of the source material of the specific traditions.

THE THIRD TURNING: THE RESTORATION

The third turning of the Gnostic wheel incorporated the fruits of scholarly works laid down after the discoveries at Nag Hammadi, and united the life-giving knowledge that comes from the living source of the Mystery, namely Man.

The ideology of Universalism was broken when the world witnessed what unconscious obedience could entail, as in Nazism and Communism. Secularization meant that the unity in religious belief and practice was broken up, and so gave new breeding ground for a greater degree of religious free thinking. This period has similarities with Hellenism, a Hellenism that has lost its virtue to postmodern meaninglessness, and the belief in Truth.

This era in Gnosticism can be seen as a form of rational romantic period. Sethians facing a disrobed world which has been re-enchanted on the Gnostic initiates' own terms.

One can consciously rehabilitate pleasant clichés, for example; enjoying red wine by a fireplace in the company of friends. Even though we know that the conceptualization of "fireplace and friends" is a culturally acquired composition that forms a network of cognitive structures in the mind, providing premises for what belongs to, and what does not belong to the situation.

Those who are within the paradigm of the Restoration have a modern understanding of the consequences of cognition, using the functional sides of the old forms and the old costumes as a vehicle for their teachings.

One of these communities, which is important for this book, is the *Sodalitas Sanctum Seth* (SSS).

This Gnostic community is both modern and close to the original ideas of the Sethian school, as it might have been in the time 300 BC to 300 AD. The reason behind this claim is that SSS built on the historical and textual foundations of the Sethian tradition, in harmony with its presented form.

SSS is a living tradition that was built on the parts that are known in the original Sethian material and filled the gaps in the doctrine based on sources that have been available through participation in various closed societies. The main source is however, now and then, the individual experience of the Mystery. Thus modern Sethians are heirs to the Mystery and its traditional practices, as modern expressions of the Sethian Masters of old.

To provide insight into this tradition's use of the Sethian tale, the author has been permitted by courtesy of the SSS to reproduce one of the traditional sources, which will be the subject of the interpretative keys in this book.

Through the Restoration, one of the Sethian tradition's prophecies is fulfilled, as indicated in *The Book of the Great Invisible Spirit:*

Seth hid his teachings on the mountain Charaxio, so he could return to his descendants and ensure that the redemptive doctrine did not leave the world before the end of time.

The Book of Eleleth

The Sethian Story
of
Sodalitas Sanctum Seth

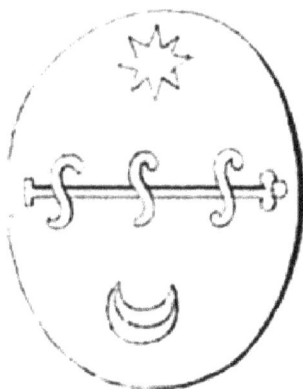

The vision in the Chapel

Late one evening when I was sitting alone in the Chapel of the Four Luminaries, the Holy Spirit came over me and covered me in a Golden Cloud. When I gave way to the perfect rapture, I heard a wonderful voice coming to me from all sides. I opened my soul's lips, and my heart asked the loneliness: Who are you? And the voice answered and said:

"I am true Light, Light that dissolves the darkness of the heavenly velvet night. I am the force that pulls the veil aside for those who live in the kingdom of the warring forces. I am the Light that glows, that warms or devours. To you, I am what you might recognize and comprehend in the Abode of Darkness, but rise now and see me with the eyes of the Man of Light, and you will see me as Eleleth, the guide from the Fullness in this abode, and you will realize that you are Seth and Christ, Father and Mother, the indivisible unity. As I am one with the Father, so are you one with me."

He reached to me with his hands. The left was as covered by bright peacock feathers, and the right as the doves' winter plumage.

He then said: "Be thou innocent as the dove and as cunning as the snake, and I will guide you, and the angel in you, on the paths of revelation."

He then said: "The light was moving. Darkness came to be. Search and you shall find, for the truth is wrapped in the very cradle of lies."

I felt an infinite urge for freedom, union, and love and the Infinite realm. And the Great Light said:

"The door is the broken heart and the key is the reconciled mind."

"I will teach you the truth about your origin and the creation of the Aeons; but only if you listen as a Living being will you be able to hear my words, for the Light is for the Light and darkness for the darkness."

Suddenly, I was released from my abode and in the Light I experienced the beginning, even though my body never moved from the place I was seated.

THE ORIGIN

The Origin of Origins, is a perfect, fulfilled and indivisible entity. It is neither he nor she, as no such category can grasp It. It is all qualities in perfect unity and harmony, nothing is missing, nothing needed, and nothing requested. It is the perfect rest in which It contemplates Its nature in the great silence, in the Light surrounding It, which is the source of the Living Water of Light. It is a being, yet not a being as we usually perceive a being. It is boundless in Its being for in It there is no limit, no centre and no extent. It is like an eternity in an eternity; It is God and the origin of all. It is The Great Invisible Spirit which is above all that is, was, and ever shall be.

It has no part in the Aeons nor in time. It does not exist in anything lower or higher than himself, since everything is in It. But he is united with them all.

It has no name, as no one was before it to give it a name; It is perfect, eternal, unknown.

It is God, the imperishable and pure Light. It is the invisible Spirit, and cannot be compared to a god, or any such thing. The Invisible Spirit or Being is more than a god, as gods might be described or understood.

It is Life that leads to Life; It is the Infinite filling Infinity. It is Knowledge that gives Knowledge.

Those who try to describe the Invisible Spirit have never succeeded in describing It. Therefore, what can I say about the Origin?

One can say nothing about Its being without restricting It to a lie and describing something other than first intended.

It is the Origin of all the Aeons. It sees Itself by watching the forms as they were in the beginning. It directs Its passion towards the Light-Water in itself which is the Source of the infinite Life of The Fullness.

THE MOTHER

Its motion became a reality, and the Providence of all came to be in the Light-Water as the Mother of all. Her Light is like Its Light. She is the unerring power, who is the living image of the invisible, perfect virginal Spirit.

She is Barbelo, the first being of the Origin, and she took part in Its being. She praised the Invisible Spirit because She had come to being through It, and Its Light-Water.

This is the first thought. She is the Motherly womb of all things, for She is the first. She is the Mother-Father, the first Man, the Holy Spirit, the Male-Female, the first who came to Be.

Barbelo is one with the Origin, even as they separated, and their eternity was filled with Aeons in Silence.

Barbelo asked for five major Aeons, with their companions, to fill Her being with qualities, and Her will became a reality in their union:

Thought and Spirituality
Fore-thought and After-thought
Immortality and Resurrection
Eternal Life and Form
Truth and Prophecy

This became the Pentad in Aeon of the Origin, which are the qualities of the Holy Spirit in the Mansions of Silence.

They are five double forces which together are One and None. They stood up and praised Barbelo and The Invisible Spirit, who are the source of their origin in which they now took part.

THE SON

After Barbelo completed this work; the Great Invisible Spirit gazed into Barbelo with the Light-Water that surrounds It, and She conceived by It an indescribable, incomprehensible Light, and this Light became the only begotten Son of the Mother-Father. He is the Light of Lights. He is the Divine Autogenes.

In Its ineffable Love, the Invisible Spirit anointed Its only begotten with his Love, until he became perfect in its Fullness.

The Only Begotten stood before the Origin, and while the Light-Water flooded over him; he, now Christ, praised the Invisible Spirit and Barbelo whereby he had come into being.

He asked His origin for the gift of Gnosis, and Gnosis became his companion.

This is the creation which was fulfilled in the Silence, this is the Holy Trinity, and is thus known because they truly are One in Three, not three in one.

The Four Lights

Gnosis was great and gave rise to the Will and the Word, and these constituted the movement and being of the Son.

Through the Fivefold Power of the Holy Spirit, and the Gnosis of the Christ, and through His Will and Word, which speak the silent language of the Father, Four Lights came into being:

The first light is Armozel; in Armozel is Charis (Grace), Aletheia (Truth) and Morph (Form).

The second light is Oriael; in Oriael is Katabole (Reflection), Aisthesis (Insight) and Mnem (Recollection).

The third light is Daveithai; in Daveithai is Dianoia (Understanding), Philios (Love) and Idea (Imagination).

I am the fourth light which is Eleleth; and in me is Katartisis (Perfection), Eirene (Peace) and Sophia (Wisdom).

These are The Twelve Aeons, which stand before the Son.

They all came into being through Him and the will of the Holy Spirit. The Fullness of the Pleroma is in these Aeons. They are one with the Son just as the Son is one with the Father. They constitute a movement and a rest, and an infinite existence.

MAN

By the united will of the Pleroma, the Perfect Man came to be a manifestation of all previous stages of the emanation. Barbelo called him Pigera-Adamas and put His consciousness over the first Aeon, Armozel, in union with the Christ. His powers were with him, and he praised the Fullness for his creation and for the Gnosis that was with him, in Christ and the Holy Spirit.

Pigera-Adamas installed Christ's consciousness, who is Seth, in the second aeon, Oriael.

In the third Aeon was Seth's offspring; these are the souls of the Saints, and they live with and in Daveithai.

In the fourth Aeon, He put me, the Fourth Light Eleleth, so that I could guide and develop Pigera-Adamas' children to the fulfillment of their understanding of the consequences of their Gnosis. This was done so that their will should continue the Pleroma's fulfillment of the All, thus assuring its internal unity with the Origin.

These are the beings who praised the Invisible Spirit through movement.

Eleleth pointed to the abodes of eternity and said:

"Everything that came to be, came to be in Unity, Fullness, and Harmony, where unity and diversity are the same. This is a state that is incomprehensible if you have not seen it, as I have shown you now."

I gazed into the Eternity, and was filled with an indescribable unity. This experience occurred so suddenly, it was as if I had forgotten that I have always been in this state of unity. Then I was filled with grief over my own state and that of all the people in the world. How distant this state seemed to be from the worldly life; yet it is never farther than a heartbeat away.

Then Eleleth took hold of me with its twin-coloured hands, and said:

"What I have shown you will never leave you, and you will, for the rest of your life, search for it in everything you see and in everything you hear in the world. You will not find a place of rest on earth, but this very search will be the cause of your redemption."

THE FALL

Eleleth said: "Sophia was in my eternity, as Barbelo in motion, and as the Holy Spirit as inspiration and the flame of creativity. She stood on the cliffs of Chaos and found in herself a rising motion. This movement was not consistent with the motion initiated from the silence of the Fullness.

She created within Her a divided and torn being in the image of God. An imperfect work came out of Her. Her mind contracted, and she miscarried a pair of twins into the void, into the infinite uncreated Chaos of possibilities.

The twins were fused; they were moving and had an unstable form, like a snake with a lion's head. They had eyes like flashing bolts of lightning.

Sophia then turned away in shame, and in that movement Metanoia came to be. This happened for the aid of all those who would be led astray because of the fruits of Her will. She surrounded her miscarried work with a luminous cloud and placed a throne in the middle of it, to pacify and hide him. However the being could be neither hidden nor made passive, due to the shadow of creativity within it.

On its throne, the corrupt being saw his reflection in the clouds. It saw a throne in the empty sky with a mighty Lion with blood on his mouth caused by the damage he had inflicted upon himself when he broke his own heart.

In the Darkness the reflection created a dark throne with a huge serpent that meandered in disobedience to his own thoughts.

Sophia gave the lion the name Yaldabout, and Yaldabout called his reflection Nebroel."

This is the Ruling power; he stole the unity, fullness and eternity from his mother, who was a great flowing Light. He removed himself from the Fullness and the boundaries of Silence. He made his own Aeon with a creative, consuming fire, which still exists today.

Yaldabout and Nebroel

The great angel Yaldabout contemplated the great demon Nebroel, who is also called Aponoia, or madness, his vivid reflection.

Together they led a spirit of copulation to the earth, and he made angelic hosts with his own reflection. Yaldabout had, however, received the unconscious images of the Fullness from the Light of the Mother, and they were engraved in his very being.

He said to the great demon Nebroel, "Let us create according to our desires, so that we can reign".

However, his pictures and understanding were given by his unconscious knowledge of the Fullness, through the Light of the Mother, and thus gave anything he created indications of its existence.

Yaldabout said, "Let twelve powers be created in the twelve

outer regions, as a circle of fire around our creation."

Thus the twelve were created. Again, he copulated with his image, and they created seven angels in their Aeons, to move through the twelve, and make beautiful, but meaningless patterns for the development and future of the creation.

He said to the great angels, "Go, and rule over your given part of the heavens."

The angels went, and the Zodiac was created, and they became the Rulers of Fate:

Athoth: Aries
Harmas: Taurus
Kalil-Oumbri: Gemini
Yabel: Cancer
Adonaiou Sabaoth: Leo
Cain: Virgo
Abel: Libra
Abrisene: Scorpio
Yobel: Sagittarius
Armoupieel: Capricorn
Melceir-Adonein: Aquarius
Belias: Pisces

He set Seven Kings in the seven planets, and each was set to work in the Houses of the Zodiac.

The first is Athoth, Moon
The second is Eloaio, Mercury
The third is Astafaios, Venus
The fourth is Yao, The Sun
The fifth is Sabaoth, Mars
The sixth is Adonin, Jupiter
The seventh is Sabbateon, Saturn.

The rulers united with each other and created their own angels, until they were 365 in total. They shared their dual fire with the Kings: Yaldabout's creative fire and Nebroel's consuming fire.

Yet Yaldabout would let none take part in the Light that he had taken from his mother, and which in ignorance made him their ruler.
When the light had mingled with their confusion and darkness, the darkness shone as a gloomy golden mist.
When the hosts were created, Yaldabout spoke to the spirits:
"I am a jealous God. You shall have no other gods before me."
By proclaiming this, he told the angels and demons who were with him that there were indeed other Gods, and the seeds of knowledge were planted in them as well, for the redemption of all.

Metanoia

After this, Sophia discovered that she was inside this darkness. She had been seduced by the disturbed powers into a wandering life of baseness. She turned and prayed to the fullness that her partner would come to her rescue. The Unknown stooped down, and through seals and names he brought her up through heavens and hells.

From the Aeons a voice thundered down to the ruling powers: "Man and the Son of Man exist."

Sophia could not return to her own Aeon where she once dwelt. Instead, she was restored to a place just above Yaldabout so that she could secretly guide his creation back to her Life.

Sophia Metanoia, carries forever in herself the pattern for this reintegration.

The Father gave His consent in the immovable seed of the holy restored men and women, who came from the great Seth. These individuals would plant Metanoia in the Aeons of the Rulers.

Through Sophia Metanoia, the state of deprivation, could again return into the Fullness.

Sophia Metanoia came down to the world, which was as the realm of darkness. She prayed for the Rulers in their Aeons, and for their creation.

THE CREATION OF MAN

Yaldabout and his angels gazed down into the shining water of the abyss, and in it they saw the reflection of the Divine Man in the Fullness. And the desire arose in them to own this being.

Yaldabout said: "Let us make man in our image so that his image may be a light for us".

Yaldabout called forth all the ruling powers to create a soul-being in the image they had seen. It was to be a creature of the zodiacal and planetary powers of angels and demons, locked together in codes, symbols and secret names.

They said, "Let us call him Adam, so that his name shall be a lantern for us".

But the man remained a lifeless image.

MAN AND THE FULLNESS

Sophia saw this, and longed again to lead her Light back into the Fullness, so that it once more could partake of its Unity.

The Mother's messenger said to Yaldabout:

"Breathe your Spirit into your human creature's face and his nature will be vital and full of life."

Then Yaldabout blew into him, but this breath was the Spirit of his Mother which he had withheld from all of his creation except this lifeless body in the image of Man.

And this was how the Light of the Fullness, and the source of unity was blown into the human being, but man did not understand it. The powers in him were as veils and labyrinths in his mind. The being began to move, and it shone in its vast, but hidden force, for in him the whole Fullness was hidden. The powers saw this and grew envious. This human creature was their work, and they had given their power to it, but his perfection was greater than theirs, and even greater than that of the first Ruler.

When they saw the uniqueness of the human being, they threw it wrathfully into the darkest parts of their creation, and the Light of man shone in the darkness, but the darkness comprehended it not.

The seeds of the Fullness are at rest in humanity, and the Mother and all of the Fullness, with its angels and beings support Man.

When the Rulers saw that Man was still shining and superior to them, they took fire, air, water and earth and forged it together in an unnatural way. They made a weak material body as clothing or a container for the Man of Light and its soul. And there, in the abodes of darkness they bound it together in hatred and anger. Then they filled mankind with material desire, the fear of the unknown, and induced the yoke of death upon it.

However, this did not change the true nature of Man but they made it more difficult for it to access its true consciousness and being.

It was Yaldabout's loss of the Light he stole from his mother, that began the war in the heavens. The battle between Yaldabout's angels and Nebroel's demons. Nebroel would not be ruled and guided by a force that was not greater than her own.

This war is now a battle that is fought in the unconscious mind of Mankind, as enslaved gladiators fought to the death for strange and foreign Kings and Princes.

ADAM, EVE AND THE SERPENT

In the lower parts of being, on the border between heaven and hell, lies the world. In this sphere Yaldabout created the Garden of Eden as a prison for his creation, Man. Here all of Adam's needs would be met so he would not try to escape. He would have no reason to look inwardly into the core of himself, thus being able to discover his origin and true nature.

The pleasures given him were bittersweet, and their beauty led to bewilderment. The pleasure was deception, the trees were made of materialism, and the fruit was a sweetly intoxicating poison, its end: death and forgetfulness.

The Tree of Life, which Yaldabout had planted in the middle of the garden, is in reality the tree of *their* life. The root is sour, the branches corruption, in its sap hatred flows, and the leaves cover the spirit of the sun creating deceptive shadows. From the flowers came ointments of drowsiness, its fruit is addiction, vile lust is in its seeds, and they sprout in spiritual darkness.

The Tree of Knowledge is of a different character. The fruit of this tree is the knowledge of good and evil, but also of dream and reality, which marks the border between truth and falsehood; light and darkness. The Ruling powers could not remove the tree, but they watched it, and warned Man against it on pain of death and punishment. In this way they sought to prevent Adam from seeking out its fruit and thus kept him from realizing his mental nudity.

The rulers perceived the Light of the Mother in Adam and desired to remove it from him by splitting him, and they took a rib from his side. Instead of removing the Light, the division created Eve, who became the earthly manifestation of the Divine Mother. Both have the same Fullness in them, as water split in two still remains water.

Then the Mother's agent went to the snake at the base of the Tree of Knowledge. The serpent spoke with the truth of the Word, and invited Man to eat of the fruit and drink its nectar, so that they would wake up from the darkened sleep.

The woman took the fruit, ate and drank, and gave it to the man, who ate and drank, and their eyes were opened and they turned and saw the light that shines in darkness.

Eleleth then turned toward the future and said, "This practice was continued by Jesus in the Eucharist, for the slumbering man, who eats and drinks of Him, will come to know himself".

When Yaldabout understood that his Man had come to himself, he cursed Nebroel, for he believed that the snake was her agent. He called her Satan, the adversary, and Yaldabout cursed the earth he had created with Nebroel, and all that was on it. He threw the man and the woman out of the Garden of Eden, and set them out upon the earth to be chastised and punished.

CAIN, ABEL AND SETH

While they lived on earth Nebroel came and mated with Eve.
She gave birth to a dark son, whom she named Cain. He was a
son of the field. He was a walker of desert places and he knew all
the arts of the earth.

Without knowing the origin of Cain, Yaldabout stepped down
and mated with Eve. She became pregnant again and gave birth
to a white son, Abel. Abel was a man of the law and sought to
control the fields through a restrictive authority.

Cain had children with Nebroel's daughters and Abel with
Yaldabout's and they spread over the face of the earth and mated
with each other.

Cain and Abel could have nourished the Light inherited
from their parents but instead they became overshadowed
with confusion. Abel was overwhelmed by Yaldabout's self-
righteousness, and Cain by Nebroel's rebellious spirit.

Cain sacrificed crops and Abel sacrificed blood. They both lacked
the ability to realize that these offerings were not increasing their
knowledge or familiarity with the Fullness.

Yaldabout stood forth as God, and acknowledged the bloody
sacrifice of Abel but not the fruits of the field that Cain tended.
Thus Cain became flooded with Nebroel's rebellious anger and
murdered Abel.

Yaldabout heard Abel's blood calling to him from the field. He
wanted to punish Cain with inhuman suffering, but instead, he
decided to put Nebroel's mark on him and his family with the
provision that no one shall kill or harm anyone with the mark.
Yaldabout wanted Cain's family to remain forever forlorn
wanderers of the earth as fallen angels in a world without
meaning or Light.

Yaldabout also decided that Abel's descendants were to be his chosen people. Thus he could tame them to be his perfect subjects through his law. He remained ignorant of the fact that the blood of Abel had already been mixed with the offspring of Cain.

After all of this was fulfilled, Eve united herself with Adam and conceived Seth.

Seth was thus the unification of the qualities of the Father and the Mother. Seth was golden, a perfect Man in the darkness of matter, and his female counterpart was Horaia. Seth is both united and separated from the Fullness, the true Man in the Fullness. He received Gnosis through Adam and his Metanoia.

As Christ, Seth spoke to his hidden nature about the plan of the Fullness; to release the captive Light in the man of earth. Thus, Seth was filled with the Holy Spirit and became the being called Christ on earth.

He dressed in the black cloak of a wanderer which would become the distinctive symbol of his people. He then obtained the experience and characteristics of Cain and Abel. By receiving the brand of Nebroel, the mark of Cain, Seth would receive Nebroel's support. Seth also learnt the laws of the creator and reaped the favour of Yaldabout as well. He brought with him the redeeming Mystery of the Fullness into the world. As an act of merciless love, he the first initiator, sent his children to fulfill the Great Work with the man of clay.

In order to ensure his liberation from the lower regions, Seth, enfolded in his black cloak, went invisibly into the Garden of Eden. In a cloud of light he passed the cherubim's sword to find the Tree of Life. There he fetched a seed and planted it in the mouth of his dead father, before he was laid to rest. The seed became a tree, and from this tree was the cross of Jesus created.

Thus Seth would be freed from his material form, for the way of the descent is also the way of the ascension.

THE SEED OF THE GREAT SETH

Eleleth then showed me how Seth's offspring acted in the world. United with the Fullness, Seth prayed to the Origin and asked the Mother for the wellbeing of his kin.

Seth's people had spread across the world to follow their father's precepts and their capital seat was in Sodom and Gomorrah.

This is the source of the great immovable race, those who know the Fullness. This is the great immovable race, who have been transformed by the actualization of their Light. They are no longer of this world, neither of Cain nor of Abel's race. These people have dissolved the horizontal mirror image of Yaldabout and Nebroel, and the vertical distortion of the Pleroma in this world.

This is the race of sacred men and women who secretly redeem the world through cunning and Gnosis.

Yaldabout wants to destroy the Children of Seth

When Yaldabout discovered the people of Seth among the inhabitants of the kingdom, redeeming humankind and returning them to the Fullness, he wanted to destroy mankind to be rid of this unwanted seed, lest he lose all control over his creation.

To destroy the sons and daughters of Seth, a great flood was sent to mark the end of an era. But the Sethians survived.
Because of this generation, firestorms tormented the world, but the kin was shown mercy through the warnings of prophets and guardians who led them to safety.
Because of this generation, there will be temptations and lies of false and confused prophets and only those who have awoken to reality can stand against them.
The great Seth saw what Yaldabout had done, the many guises and masks and the schemes against the immovable race. He also saw how the treacherous forces and angels joined Yaldabout to expose and destroy his race.
Seth asked for guardians to protect his family and the Mother sent Angels of the Son from the great Aeons. All these Angels are one with the Son in the Pleroma. They have continued to protect the immovable seed to this very day, its people and its workings; and they will continue to protect them until the end of the world.

Seth as Jesus

To enhance the execution of the plan, the Pleromatic Seth descended according to the will of the Great Invisible Spirit, and carried with him the Five Seals which are the Keys of the Fullness. Through words and actions he would teach people how they could liberate themselves from the power of the Rulers. He would thus make his entire life a living demonstration of this.

Seth experienced three events: birth, awakening in a human body and the wrath of the Rulers. He did this to redeem men and women who had been lost since the creation of the world, and to strengthen the seed in their teachings and knowledge of the Mystery.

This was done through the baptism of a worldly body, a body that Seth prepared for himself mysteriously through a virgin.

He came to earth as a teacher so that people could learn to receive the Holy Spirit and grow through Her.

He would guide them through secret symbols.

He would guide them through the dissolution of the world without dissolving himself.

He would guide them through sacraments and ceremonies.

He would guide them through devotion to the Holy and Immovable, the Heart of the Father, and the Great Light which existed before they came to be in the Providence.

SETH ESTABLISHES THE BAPTISM

When Jesus understood his true nature to be Seth, he began his work in the world. He instituted holy baptism, surpassing the heavens through providence. Through the amniotic fluids of the Jordan, he had entered in to become the Living Jesus.

He taught teachings of the Light to those who had ears to hear and clear perception to see.

He healed the deaf and prepared the generations through teachings and rituals that he would leave as his inheritance. After some time the Rulers ignorantly assisted him in disrobing the man that covered him.

He has opened a door that is not a door. Thus he has revealed a path through the mirror for those who are sent in and out. He equips them with the armour of the truth and of the Mystery and with a moving and invincible force.

SETH'S MESSAGE TO HIS DESCENDANTS

About this door is heard the sound of the heavens singing, conveying the message of Seth from the heights of Charaxio.

"I am Seth, the first Man in the eternity of the Fullness.

I am the moving reality of the Origin.

I am the Son of Barbelo and the anointed Autogenes.

I am crowned with the Four Luminaries, and in Me is the beginning and end.

With Me are life and light, liberty and love which are the conditions for realizing the Mystery.

I am the Father of Life and the Key to its door. Through baptism and anointment I will awaken you from your sleep and lead you to the Life. For as I am one with the Father, so are you one with me. Therefore, take up your crosses and follow me, and do to the sleeping humanity as I have done to you.

One God, One Man, and One Infinite Existence." Amen.

The end of the vision

When I walked through the door, I was once again in the chapel and He was with me. He baptized me with the Fivefold baptism, and showed me the seals and the names that open the gates of Chaos, the Universe, and the Heavens. This he did so that the Mystery would be preserved on earth, among brothers and sisters of the secret chapel, those who are surrounded by the black cloak. They are the pilgrims of the soul and the hidden initiators of a sleeping mankind.

The angel showed me another symbol and said: This is the seal of the sanctuary for those who seek to enter it. By the right understanding of this symbol, Metanoia will meet the seeker at the outer gates of the Mystery.

Finally, he said: "Be wise as a serpent and innocent as a dove in your workings and save yourself no effort, because the spirit of redemption will be with you in everything you do."

The light disappeared and I found myself alone in the Chapel of the Four Luminaries. I immediately wrote down all the things I had experienced. I united with the Man of Light and began the labour that Seth had imposed upon us.

This is the book of Amarantus delivered by Seth
through the Holy Angel Eleleth.
Heli Heli Machar Machar Seth

Sethian keys of interpretation

In order to understand the meaning of these Sethian stories, the reader will need a key for interpretation. In this chapter we will introduce some of these keys. They are described here in psychological-religious terms, even though they also constitute an infinite macrocosmic spiritual dimension.

It is not the intention of the author to simplify the story, but to render it understandable. Therefore, there are also keys which will not be explained here.

The author will not try to unveil the story but rather point in the general direction of the Mystery, by giving these keys, so that those who seek may find.

The keys will provide a background for contemplating the story's underlying meaning.

The Origin

The Origin or the Great Invisible Spirit is the narrative expression of the true God, or the Father. God is in all ways indescribable, since God is everything and nothing. God is not a he or a she, and has no personality or name. In this way God can almost be described as an intelligent form of Nirvana.

God's extension, from the point without a centre, is called the Fullness or Pleroma, and it Is all that Is. There is little focus on the Father, as it is impossible to describe an indescribable being who is beyond comprehension.

The Origin

THE HOLY SPIRIT

Sethian tradition describes the Holy Spirit as a feminine being. This should not be understood in the narrow sense, i.e. that She is female or a goddess. This is because gods and goddesses belong to the created world, and are thus expressions of Yaldabout and Nebroel. The Holy Spirit appears in many different guises, since Her reality provides various forms of being in the Aeons that emanate from Her. Presented below are some of the manifestations of the Holy Spirit. The Holy Spirit is, next to the Father, the being in the Sethian story which is most difficult to describe. She has many characteristics and functions with an inner and hidden unity. The distinct features describing her here are limited to those represented in *The book of Eleleth*.

Barbelo:
Barbelo is the mind of God, and is the highest possible conceivable existence, bordering on the incomprehensible. Barbelo is closely connected to the Origin. One could say that She, who is also masculine, is the first manifestation of God which can be conceived. She is like unto an eternity. It is therefore a common claim that Barbelo is the actual God of Sethianism. There are several interpretations of the word Barbelo. One of these interpretations is "the Son of Man", for she can be described as the true Man; not mankind as we know it, for She is self-consciousness without borders.

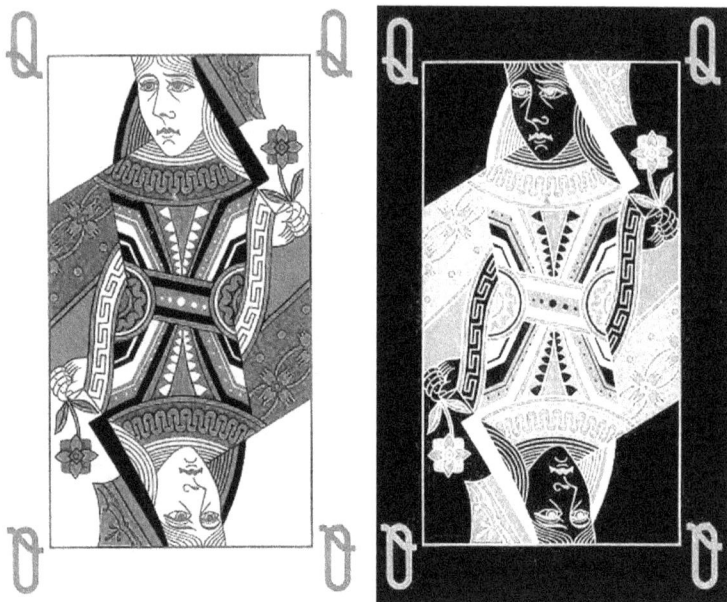

The Holy Spirit

Sophia:

Sophia means wisdom, and important aspects of her are inspiration and creativity. She also represents these qualities in all people. It was through inspiration, detached from the divine plan, that she created the ego, which is Yaldabout. However, it is through the same door by which we came into the world that we may exit. After her restoration from her fall, Sophia works as the initiator of the world.

She stands on the threshold between Pleroma and the distorted image. She stands at the junction between here and there. She is the crossroads, the limbo, the man in the no man's land.

Here, she is a messenger for self-knowledge and an exporter of the understanding needed to break free, so as to once again live a life of wholeness and fullness. She is the connection between the ego and the higher or divine self.

Sophia-Prunikos:

The lowest manifestation of the Holy Spirit is the *Sophia-Prunikos*. She is Sophia as a drunken harlot who has only partial access to the truth and has no direction in her being. She is an entity that moves from predator to predator in search of whatever she sees as meaningful at the time.

This aspect of Sophia is the image of the spiritually weak-minded man or woman who has not experienced what might lead to the recognition of his or her true nature. This true nature is discovered in the meeting with Metanoia. It should be noted that without Sophia-Prunikos, Metanoia would have no purpose.

Metanoia:

Metanoia represents the spiritual turning point, giving rise to a new understanding of the world. She is an experience which best can be described as a eureka moment. It is impossible to approach Gnosis gradually, just as one cannot approach infinity step by step.

Sethianism may be taught step by step, but this road only leads to Metanoia. She, or it, always comes as a surprise, coming in unexpected forms and at unexpected times.

If the visit is announced, the visitor is never Metanoia.

Three manifestations:

There are several different archetypes of contradicting images of the Holy Spirit's work. These can be seen in Sethianism as Mary Magdalene, the Virgin Mary, and Lilith: from Seth's genealogy comes Mary Magdalene, from Abel's family the Virgin Mary, and from Cain's family Lilith, who might be perceived as the shadow of the Holy Spirit, even if this in itself is a paradox.

Seth, Christ and Jesus

"In him was life; and the life was the light of men.
And the light shineth in darkness; and the darkness
comprehended it not".
The Gospel of John

The Son appears in many guises. He is the Anointed one of the Origin, the Self-created (Autogenes), Seth and Christ. All these are the same character but with different functions in various situations, environments and spheres of activity. Just as a man has different roles in life: employee, father, soldier, head of the house, lover etc., but still remains the same individual.

The manifestations of the Son are all closely connected to redemption; even before there existed anything to redeem. The Son is the ability to dissolve the works that came into being after the creation of Barbelo.

In order to be a redeemer for Humanity, He must also be a dissolver of the world, which cannot exist without the Light of the Fullness.

This is also his actual function after the creation of the world of matter.

Of all the people born on earth there are two prominent and well-known manifestations of the Son: Seth, the son of Adam and Eve, and Jesus of Nazareth. Alongside these were also Mechizedek, called Zorakatora, and others. We will however not go into their function here. It is Seth and Jesus that this book presents, and these two lived their lives as revelations of the Son on earth, according to the myth, and has thus initiated the reintegration process in all people.

Reintegration describes the integration process of the Light back into the Fullness.

The Son

All manifestations of the Son have been initiators in the sense that they have paved new ways to Gnosis, traditions to be followed after their human form was destroyed.

One could say that what the Son did, in his physical form, was to aid spiritual development by communicating to a resourceful few a spiritual art of survival. To continue the metaphor, these individuals initiated others in the same ways, by teaching them sustainable spiritual development. Additional help and mental rations are flown in to this disaster area, as visions, dreams, insights, and direct guidance from the Pleroma.

The life of the historical Jesus is not the most central part of Sethianism, but his teachings and actions constitute a mixture of human and divine actions; as Seth or Christ, also known as Aberamento, came to the world in and through the body of Jesus. He came to teach the way of redemption and to re-establish contact between mankind and the Holy Spirit.

Between God and mankind, is the Cross, which in Sethianism is an important symbol. Only those who take up their cross and follow Christ will be able to break the barrier that keeps man trapped in the material universe. This occurs through a paradox, the clock's thirteenth hour, which is the door in the sky.

A vigilant eye is needed in the reading of Gnostic texts. One must be able to separate the wheat from the chaff, for no man can perform all actions in accordance with truth. This is a truth the writers of the canonical gospel did not understand, or may have refused to accept. No man or woman dwells in constant unity with the Fullness, yet they portray the entire life of Jesus as the very life of God Himself.

Inside man, Christ is the redemptive process which dissolves unhealthy bonds and circular patterns, and forms the basis for a psychological non-attachment. The Sethian rests in himself, in communion with the perfect Silence of the Fullness.

MAN

"And the Gnosis of the Light was hidden in Adam"
The secret book of John

The human being is the core mystery of the Sethian tradition as well as in most other Gnostic traditions. Each individual possesses all the qualities described in *The book of Eleleth*.

The human composition:
The relationship between Man, the divine and the fallen world is the basis for all theology and practice in the Sethian system. The human being, created by the Rulers, is made in the divine image, and therefore has similar qualities in its body and soul. It is through Sophia, who is Barbelo on a lower arch, that the fallen man is connected to the first and true man. This is a great mystery, which requires not only analysis but also familiarity with the inner life of the Gnostic story.

Material men and women, who live on the earth, are composed of body, soul and spirit.

The Spirit is Barbelo, the true man.

The physical body is composed of the four elements, and serves as a garment (or a straitjacket) for the spirit of Man. It limits us and requires continuous care, and even then this form is doomed to perish. In this world of reflections people see and feel the body and believe it to be the real being of man, unaware that it is the hidden Man of Light that is our true nature.

Man

The body has as little to do with our true nature, as a liquid with the cup into which it is poured. The body has no innate positive or negative value; it is neutral. From an eternal perspective the body is only a part of the human experience, including polarities such as joy and suffering.

Sethians consider the body as a tool, a being they possess, in the same manner as you may have a pet dog. It is important to treat it well so it does not suffer, because if it suffers, it may attract undesired attention. It is critical to both train and restitute the body so that its animal inclinations can be held in check. Last but not least, it is important to reward the body. How this is done is up to the individual to decide, according to one's personal preferences.

The point is in all cases that the body is not sinful or evil. It is a companion, and is to follow the instructions of the higher self of the individual. How to use it beyond this is up to individual taste.

On the spiritual level, the body may reveal secrets about the creation, the Rulers, and their nature, just as knowledge of genetic material may say something about our physical conditions.

The soul may be described as the place where matter and spirit meet and are fused together. The stories tell us that it is made with a web of archetypes, such as those found in Astrology. In its developed form it will provide spiritual insights through words, thoughts and images into the material world.

The soul is a structure that must be led by the spirit, lest it be tormented by the Rulers and the Demons. It is drawn between the legislator and the lawless, and is consigned to one of them, if one indulges one of them. This means that if you indulge in one of the religious forms of the demiurge, you will enter into some sort of connection to one of the aspects of Yaldabout.

74

It is also through materialism and worship of aspects of the world that humans make a similar connection to Nebroel. In both cases, one gives away one's mental and emotional freedom in return for a life of service to a deity that has very few merits when it comes to the love for mankind.

Participation in the spiritual warfare against the enemies of one's god will fill these people with experiences of meaning and mystery, and they will consider their position as good and that of the opponent as evil. This might provide a warped sense of meaning to even the most meaningless defeats in life.

It is, however, said that the healed soul is the chalice of spiritual wine and that the perfected human is a stranger to the Rulers.

The soul is part of both the problem and the solution. The soul is, according to the tradition, a very complicated organism. It has led us to the world, but yet it contains the tools of redemption.

The soul is used as a vehicle, in the sacrament of Ascension, which consists of journeys through spiritual worlds and Aeons. Through the experiences on these journeys, knowledge of the spiritual abodes is gained, and through this knowledge, the Great work may be fulfilled.

HUMAN TYPES

One of the most controversial aspects of the Gnostic doctrine of Man, is the classification of human traits into three types. These types are rough categories that will help the initiator or Gnostic to determine where in the educational training system any individual should begin their learning. It is not intended to be a system for evaluating the worth of people, but to ensure that those seeking the tradition will be able to access the next step within their individual growth.

In Valentinianism the taxonomy is linear and vertical, and has the correspondences shown in the table below:

The Valentinian model:

Type	Faculty	Son of Adam and Eve
Pneumatic	Spirit	Seth
Psychic	Mind	Abel
Hylic	Body	Cain

The reason for this linear form of Valentinian theory is that it postulates that Abel is better off than Cain, as the Demiurge is better than Satan. Since one of the Valentinian projects was to reconcile Pistic Christianity with Gnostic Christianity, this model of ranking is a result of the influence of the dawning New Testament Christianity.

The Pneumatics are dominated by the spirit, and exceed good and evil. The Pneumatic is delivered by living his understanding of his true nature and it is this perspective that is conveyed in this book.

The Psychic is dominated by archontic structures and the struggle between good and evil, right and wrong. The Psychics experience fulfilment by dedicating themselves to law, norms and customs. They seek to follow the way of the Demiurge and will dwell in his Aeon to the end of time, when the consummation of everything will take place.

The Hylic is dominated by materialism and the values of the world and is not willing to play by the rules of the Demiurge, and thus they take part in Nebroel's abode.

To conclude the above, the soul is neither bad nor good, but might be a container for both. For the redeemed human, it is the vehicle of the spirit and the Man of Light. The Sethian is a spiritual acrobat and a master in the art of living. He does not take part in structures which limit his freedom to the cognitive cages of the Rulers.

The consequences for the three personality types are therefore as follows:

The soul is to the Psychic, what the spirit is for the Pneumatic, yet the Psychic considers them to be the same thing.

A Pneumatic cannot 'sin', as the concept of sin ceases to exist in the moment of realization of the consequences of the Mystery.

Therefore, Hylics sin in everything they do, as they do not possess the Mystery and are unable to relate to the truth. This means that they might turn into Yaldabout's unconscious slaves. They might escape his regime, by systematic disobedience, but then stand in danger of being consumed by Nebroel's anarchistic nature. Hylic people will in any case be dictated by the rules or by their needs and desires, which may be the same thing. This may, at best, be of no consequence to their development or, at worst, lead to greater spiritual depravity.

Psychics are people who live in the middle; they do not know the truth, but recognize its reflections, which are good and evil.

The Psychics try to do 'good' in spite of the fact that this also confirms the existence of evil. Psychic individuals are moral individuals that live via rules and regulations learned from the experience of the structures.

Ultimately, life as a Pneumatic depends largely upon living a lucid and conscious life. It is founded on awareness, and the clarity of mind and being to know what may lead to increased spiritual gravity, of what restricts one's reality and the choices in that reality.

The Valentinian perspective on the three types has been the focus in this chapter. The Sethian perspective was presented in *The Book of Eleleth*, and will be explained below in the chapter: Cain, Able and Seth.

To conclude the description of man, some more light has to be shed on the concept of the Man of Light:

The Man of Light is the true Man within man, which is the Light of Sophia. It is important to distinguish the light from the darkness in one's own being. To do this one must acquire Gnosis, as the Sethian understanding of light and darkness is not to be understood as good and evil in the Biblical sense of the words.

Sethians must be able to identify their Cainite and Abelian dispositions, so that the true Man might appear. The Man of Light dwells within carnal man, as a red hot coal in the ashes. It requires the breath of the Holy Spirit, so that the spark may flare up, and enflame the whole being.

Many who have met Metanoia, have experienced the Man of Light, as a firefly in a jar. It can move, but not escape.

The light shines in the darkness…

The Abode of the Wise

"Behold, I send you forth as sheep in the midst of wolves: be ye
therefore wise as serpents, and innocent as doves."
The Gospel of Matthew

Another controversial topic within Gnosticism is what
Catholicism calls the communion of Saints, somewhat similar
to what Buddhism calls Bodhisattvas. It is said that those who
have fulfilled the Mystery can become the voluntary servants of
the divine love.

In Gnostic tradition it is taught that particular teachers may
still be available after they have left their earthly form. The most
developed version of these teachings is the Valentinian approach,
which is closely knit together with the ideas of redemption, and
these theories are also important in Sethianism.

Any theories dealing with life after death will mostly be regarded
as unfortunate speculation. It is difficult to authenticate such
theories, and they have little value for practical and systematic
work within the redemption of oneself or others.

The myth of the Abode of the Wise is as follows: Yaldabout has
in his Aeon a heaven, as Pistic Christianity describes Heaven
or Paradise. This is a place that is reminiscent of the Garden of
Eden and is like being in a dream. In this place, the souls who
have served under Yaldabout's law are situated as 'the righteous
souls', or the zealous followers of the so-called Christian ethic.
It is said that in this sphere there is a place called the Abode of
the Wise. This might best be described as a place where Gnostic
souls go disguised as righteous souls. This is the monastery in
the Garden of Eden.

This is a state of limbo for those who do not choose to withdraw competely into the realm of Pleroma, but for humanity's sake keep the connection with the material world.

By holding on to their psychic soul they are able to move about on all levels. This corresponds to what is known as the red body in Alchemy. Therefore, this abode is also called The College of the Philosopher's Stone, and is in other traditions called The Great White Lodge.

Thus the abode of the perfect initiates is in the sphere of the demiurge (or Craftsman), where soul and spirit are connected, and where they can continue to assist those who are trapped in matter.

An important consequence of helping people to escape from the material world is that it makes it more difficult for the assistant to escape.

This myth belongs under possible articles of faith among Sethians. There are also some who believe Yaldabout is not the only one who maintains such a place in his realm but that Nebroel also has a space for those who want to hide in matter. This place is called among other things The Black Lodge. This theme will not be further discussed here, as it is not central to the current presentation of Sethianism.

SETHIAN SAVIOURS, SAINTS AND MENTORS

In Pistic religion a Saviour is often cast as a person with supernatural powers, who is kind to his fellow men and women. Saviours open the door to heaven by for example dying for the sins of mankind, or by giving them a redeeming law.

A saint or holy person is frequently described as a person who has or had extraordinary capabilities to perform miracles in the world before and/or after his death, and who has led an exemplary religious life. In Pistic traditions teachers are people who are well schooled in the doctrine of their tradition and can convey this properly to other believers.

Within Sethianism this is quite different; a Sethian mentor is a secret wandering passage out of the mental limitations of the world.

The Sethian master is a saviour who through his or her work is a saint and a hierophant; that is one who reveals the sacred. The Sethian mentor may have formal students, which is the traditional way of conveying the teachings and mysteries.

Yet, on the other hand, everyone that interacts with such a mentor is also unknowingly his or her student. The reason for this is that the masters of the Sethian tradition regard any interactions as opportunities to initiate liberating processes. This should certainly not be understood as preaching. The Master is a teacher by virtue of his or her capacity of knowing the ways of the human mind, the meaning of the Sethian myth and by being in possession of the keys to the Mystery. The Teacher is a Master in the sense that he or she is capable of using these tools to open the eyes of the sleeping by introducing them to unexpected experiences, curious stories, and new perspectives.

How this is done depends on many circumstances, but common to them all is that it is done through the guidance of the great Mother, who is providence and wisdom. It should also be mentioned that the process of redemption is not governed by any ethical or cultural framework, as it focuses on what is needed; it is thus independent of what is culturally acceptable or *comme il faut*. It is merciless in its love, because the love for mankind controls all interactions, yet it is not always what is perceived as nice or kind that is needed in this process.

Sethian saviours do not necessarily possess special powers or perform miracles, as these are linked to Yaldabout and Nebroel. They may not stand out as exemplary men or women, as the perception of what is ideal behaviour is highly dependent on the cultural context. They do not even necessarily make the world a better place, as the world as such is not their target. They are saviours in their capacity of being messengers of the Pleroma, conveying liberation through cunning and wisdom to those who are ready to receive.

The same applies to the Sethian Saints, who through their state of Gnosis and dedication to the work, promise to aid mankind until the creation of the Demiurge is reintegrated. Saints in Sethianism may thus be considered as a form of Sethian Bodhisattvas, as described in Mahayana and Vajrayana Buddhism. It is through their experience with the Mystery and their dedication to the work that these individuals can be regarded as saints, not through miracles and virtues, although such qualities often are attributed to them.

Yaldabout and Nebroel

"After the world was established, Yaldabout said to his angels:
I am a jealous God, and nothing has come to be,
except through me.
He felt sure of his nature.
Then a voice called from above, and said:
Man exists, and the Son of Man ".
The Book of the Great Invisible Spirit.

Yaldabout is the demi-creator or demiurge. He is called the Ruler, Archon, Jehovah, Saklas and Samael. He is the leader of the creative angels who formed the material universe.

It is possible that the name Yaldabout is derived from the name of the Old Testament god Jehovah, as Yao El Sabaot, which by permutation becomes Yaldabout.

In Pagan traditions the gods of time, limitation, and partly those of war and conquest all have Yaldabout's qualities. Sethians do therefore believe that Yaldabout's masks are innumerable, and that he exists in all religions and all traditions.

Yaldabout's twin, mate, and dark side is Nebroel who is also called Aponoia, which is madness.

Nebroel is described in the Biblical story as Satan and in other religions and traditions as the opponent of the creator and lawmaker.

One is a legislator, law enforcer and judge; the other a wanderer in the wilderness, an outlaw and a criminal in the eye of the other; but even so, they depend upon each other, as they define each other through their contradictions. A suitable question is, how are we to know the qualities of light, if we do not know darkness?

Yaldabout and Nebroel

They are two sides of the same coin and fight against each other. They are reason versus emotion and vice versa.

Together they constitute a broken heart where the tear has turned one half against the other. Yaldabout judges all actions, not their motive. Therefore, a Pneumatic would be deemed as an outlaw, lawful, or as a stranger. It is important for Sethians never to indulge too extensively in any of the two opposing poles. The struggle between Creator and Destroyer is a game that imprisons the human mind, leading it away from more healthy liberating perspectives and communion with the Fullness. One must seek to unite these forces so that the Sethian door can open.

Just as the Demiurge appointed himself God, the human ego appoints itself the highest authority in our being. This makes it difficult for mankind to recognize any higher being than the conformity learned by culture and the desire to satisfy our own needs. The human spirit is the prisoner of the conscience of the mind.

The struggle between the forces is a constant factor in the world and cannot be transcended on a permanent basis as long as Man is clothed in the body of flesh. Yaldabout might be interpreted as reason and the conscious mind, while Nebroel might be interpreted as emotions and the irrational. They are the day and night side of the same being.

Sethians relate to both and neither side at the same time. By selecting the unproposed third option, when presented with two, the logic of creation is broken and a paradox opens, and creates a number between 1 and 1.0.

Sethian methods have a surreal aspect which violates the foundation of a dualistic rational system.

The Sethian is in this way both Cain and Abel but united, redeemed, and recreated. Sethian initiates are therefore in possession of the qualities of both sides, and benefit from them both. By consciously being in this position of betweenness he or she remains a spiritual stranger.

Thus the Sethians say together with Jesus, "My kingdom is not of this world".

EDEN AND GEHENNA

In Sethianism the Garden of Eden is a state of mind, it is the state of total passivity and self-satisfaction. This is a state that very few people can sustain indefinitely in the world, as events in life cause an individual to constantly move from one pole to the other. This state of inconsistency is ensured by a great amount of external stimuli, instability of interests and the quest for material prosperity. It goes without saying that a continual focus on the external is important for the Rulers to keep mankind in shackles. The Sethian story tells us that Adam and Eve were placed in a restricted garden where they had unrestricted access to food, beauty and pleasure. In this way they would not seek the truth about their condition or existence.

The opposite of this state is the infernal Eden which, among other things, is called Gehenna, the place outside. Gehenna manifests itself in areas with hunger, war, and poverty, conditions which make man unable to seek the truth. Self-preservation remains the focus, and consequently leads to an outward orientation, sometimes accompanied by the adoration of gods who claim to be able to relieve suffering and satisfy one's material needs.

Adam and Eve left Eden through the Wisdom of the Serpent, and thus taught future generations how to quit this state of existence. However, the problems connected to Eden and Gehenna remain in the world, as uneven distribution of resources, human greed and overpopulation lead to competition for material wealth. Rich nations will grow the minds of their people into a state of Eden-passivity, while poor countries conceive children into a type of Gehenna-consciousness. This is a problem that exceeds all political systems, all organizations and all developmental programs.

GODS OF HEAVEN AND OF EARTH

> "Yaldabout has a great number of faces,
> and he takes advantage of them all".
> **The Secret book of John**

One important issue regarding Yaldabout and Nebroel is how to understand other gods or goddesses in monotheistic and polytheistic religions.

This is a difficult and complex question, and one should not make a universal rule for all cases. Sethians would, as a rule of thumb, view most personified gods and goddesses as different expressions of Yaldabaout and Nebroel or their angels and demons.

This does not mean that they are evil or dangerous to humans. What is dangerous is the passive acceptance of the authority of gods and goddesses, which leaves man in a state of somnambulance.

From a Sethian perspective, all gods and goddesses may be useful or good if approached in order to dissolve rigid forms in one's own being. This means that an intellectual could benefit from working with an archetype or god who represents his or her counterpart, in order to challenge the mind to dissolve parts of its self-understanding, so as to be able to move unrestrainedly between the opposites on the path that lies between them.

The gods and goddesses together with Yaldabaout and Nebroel can be regarded as rigid expressions of the true God. Just as when looking at a photograph, one imagines and projects a number of qualities on to the image due to one's own frame of reference. Thus by describing the features of a being, one will also be able to imagine its counterpart.

We give our gods and goddesses names, forms, and qualities according to our needs and fears. It is mankind who creates gods and goddesses in its own image, rather than the other way around.

Therefore, horses, if they had religious imagination, would describe their god as a mighty horse.

It is therefore more appropriate to describe God as none, rather than one, and to give praise in silence, rather than with words.

FATE

Yaldabout made the Rulers, so that they could provide order and predictability to his creation. This is allegorically described through the creation of the Zodiac and the Planets, which through the ages have been described as forces that affect life on earth through the strengthening or weakening of their relative positions on the firmament.

It is therefore not without scepticism that Sethians through the ages have watched the beautiful star clad night sky on cloudless winter nights, whilst knowing that life on earth depends on a sphere of burning gas that is several light years away. And beyond this is the endless, cold universe and a belt of planets that move relative to each other without meaning or purpose, but always with mathematical precision.

Knowledge of astrology, as used in divination, or from a magical or an archetypal point of view, are quite often part of the knowledge that the Sethian possesses. Sethians use some forms of divination in order to understand what influence of the Rulers an individual is subject to, in order to plan whether to prepare a defence or to row with the flow.

How this knowledge is used depends on whether the approach of the practitioner is primarily religious or of a psychological nature.

CAIN, ABEL AND SETH

Cain, Abel and Seth constitute three human types within Sethianism which are called the three ancestors. The word ancestors is used to point out their relatively stable character and to clarify how one may affect the others and thus their qualities. When it comes to people who lack the experience of Gnosis it is, from a Sethian perspective, equally problematic if they be Cainitic or Abelian. However, it is difficult to cultivate an unblended Sethian perspective in the world, as it might mix badly with what is regarded as normal behaviour in the context of the everyday world.

According to tradition, it is crucial to be of Sethian spiritual descent and to become this, one has to have understood the meaning of the Mystery and been inwardly transformed by its meaning.

Cain   Seth   Abel

As one of the initiators of the tradition once said, "A man who does not possess Gnosis will always sin, while one who has Gnosis will never be able to". This requires a bit more explanation to become clear.

The Man of Light is like a serpent. It can change skin, but not its inner nature. This means that the recreated Man, who has acquired Gnosis, can take advantage of both Cainitic and Abelian properties in dealing with the world. The moral and ethical standards of the Sethian are based on experiences with the living Gnosis, not on the claims of others or written rules. However, it is appropriate to follow the laws of the country one lives in, so that one does not get into situations that damage one's own or others' development, be deprived of one's physical freedom or prevent others from having the opportunity to experience redemption.

By moving the world without being moved, and being wise as serpents and innocent as doves, the Sethians are called the Immovable Race and the Children of Seth.

Redemption

Redemption is the Sethian prerequisite for a happy life in the world, and to finding the best way home, after the death of the body. Redemption is the key to unlock the chains of the soul, through the mind.

In Sethian tradition, redemption is not something that comes after one's earthly demise.

It all begins with Metanoia, or turning around. Metanoia is understood as an existential experience that something does not make sense within the created world. When meeting her, it might seem as if all explanations are hollow and structures are recognized to be meaningless when analysed. What differentiates this from a depression is that the person thinks to perceive something almost unbelievable hidden behind the smoke and mirrors.

To refer to the movie *The Matrix*, this state of unrest is related to the question: "What is the Matrix?" which robs the main character of all rest. It can be compared to feeling like your soul is itching, but then realizing that you have no idea how to scratch it, or that it was even possible to experience such a sensation.

This condition consists of a tentative theorizing about what this might be or be about; that is, creating beliefs. This is a crucial point, where an existential anxiety may accompany the exploration. If you land too early, the process might stagnate in some form of Pistisism; however, if you are able to bear the uncertainty until the obvious imposes itself upon you, Gnosis is acquired. After this, Gnosis must be used to discover the inner meaning of the difference between god and God, the image and the reality. Only then, may one attempt to comprehend the truth concerning Man.

One will then come to terms with the experience of an unknown

Redemption

God, a Fullness, behind the creator. One understands how this affects one's life in the world of matter, what Christ did through Jesus and what he did not do, and what this means for the individual, if understood correctly.

This may be done as a unifying work, for by healing one's broken heart, one also heals one's own demiurgical qualities, for the Demiurge is also an aspect of man. Cain and Abel are united through the position in the dimension between dimensions.

Thus, Yaldabout and Nebroel might also be delivered through Gnosis, and achieve reconciliation through the intercession of the Man of Light.

Humans wander, sleepwalking or awake, together in the world. The Sethian defines a person who is awake as one who has received or acquired Gnosis. Dormant people are dreaming in Yaldabout's or Nebroel's reality which forms the sleeper's world of dream or nightmare.

What we all have in common is that we are material people with a soul and the Light of the Origin hidden within us either as a realized or potential factor.

The forms are the same. All have a body, a soul composed of zodiacal and planetary imprints, or in psychological terms; biological and environmental dispositions.

The impact that the experience of Gnosis creates in an individual's life, causes him or her to wake from the dream. One perceives the processes and is therefore ready to free oneself from their unconscious influences.

Through this liberation process, the spiritual veins of the soul are no longer filled with Yaldabout's and Nebroel's essence but rather are bled and then filled with the Light-Water of the Pleroma.

In stories of the Sethian tradition concerning the creation of the Rulers and the humans, they speak of a double fire. This fire is one of creation and destruction., and it overwhelms the soul of the sleeping man and burns his cognitive forms to hardened and inflexible structures. This makes people more and more inflexible, in mind and soul, as their years go by, if it is not actively opposed.

The pain that comes with the slow destruction of the individual's previous way of living, and especially in old age, is also a product of this fire.

The form of the soul is in itself not corrupted because it is made in the image of the true Man in the Fullnes, and it will, given the appropriate circumstances, become what it truly is.

What fills the soul, metaphorically speaking, is of utmost importance.

When Gnosis is acquired, the Sethian is, metaphorically speaking, empty. He or she is in a state of existential crisis. It is this state that St. John of the Cross describes as the dark night of the soul. In this state nothing has value, nothing is appealing, exciting or inspiring, and the spiritual presence is gone. The world appears to be totally meaningless and in this numbness one can see how human and spiritual processes interact with each other.

It is in this vacuum that Gnosis occurs and causes the emptied soul structures to suddenly, or over a period of time, to be filled anew. They are not filled with the dual hardening fire. Instead they are filled by the Light-Water of the Pleroma, the holy fiery water, which is a burning water and a humid fire.

This substance and this water are the real function of the baptism. This water makes the soul once again flexible and free, and man can once again become the true Man while still in the flesh.

The Light-Water also reflects the projections of the world, and it glows like a fire. It is this quality that makes both Yaldabout and Nebroel perceive the Sethian as one of their own.

What they see is their own fire in the reflection, and in the perfect Light behind, which makes the Sethian look like their ideal ally. The curious effect of this is that the Sethian is blessed by both Heaven and Hell, while in reality he does not belong to either. This is in other words the interaction of spirit with reason and emotion. This is the mystery of the fire and the Light-Water in the world, and in the human soul. This is a mystery with many consequences and answers for those who know how to seek them.

The Sethian is thus redeemed to the extent that the world permits, through the Mystery and through having the soul filled with the Light-Water.

The body will still be a challenge through its perception of desire and suffering. However, it also contains pieces of the map and clues for how to continue to seek fulfilment.

By reading the Sethian story and trying to understand the importance of its elements within the human mind, through the keys which are given above, one may be able to comprehend parts of the reality it intends to convey. If you mix your own life story and perspectives into this study, you will not only be able to look through the Gnostic window, but discover that you actually are on the inside, looking out.

General approaches

Philosophical-Psychological Sethianism

Carl Gustav Jung (1875-1961) was the first to connect Gnosticism with contemporary psychology. He was himself very interested in Spiritual alchemy, and believed that psychology could be considered a modern development of this. Jung himself wrote a Gnostic work, called *Septem Sermones ad Mortuos* (The Seven Sermons to the Dead), and is thus referred to by some modern Gnostics as a modern Gnostic theologian.

From a non-religious point of view, Sethianism and other Gnostic schools might be understood as a form of psychology and existential philosophy of liberation.

This modern link between Gnosticism and psychology has been expedient in providing Gnostics with good descriptive concepts to interpret the processes. Concepts from Jung and Sigmund Freud, the father of psychoanalysis, are often used.

The Sethian story is from this perspective, a story about the relationship between aspects of the mind that lead to tension, and restrictive or even pathological conditions.

The Pleroma or Fullness may serve as an image of the collective super consciousness, which is humanity's archetypal common consciousness, or a healthy peaceful mind. Yaldabout represents the ego, while Nebroel represents the subconscious feelings and desires.

Through the adopting of modern psychology, Yaldabout and his Ruling powers might be said to constitute the mind's network of cognitive structures. That is to say, from a psychological point of view Yaldabout represents all understanding of our surroundings and what kind of behaviour is expected in various situations. Nebroel challenges these patterns and tempts us to break with them.

This means that Yaldabout cannot be regarded as evil, but rather as a structure that both orders our experience and limits us by defining the boundaries of what is socially acceptable. Conscience is thus an important ruler, which acts as gatekeeper between the cultural and religious understanding of right and wrong. Yaldabout's powers are more or less rigid cognitive schemas. Over time unconscious habits which are intrinsically linked with a number of other habits will become progressively more difficult to change. The rulers ensure their own perpetuation through inducing fear of transgressing the established boundaries. Fear, especially the fear of the unknown is one of the rulers' best weapons. Besides closing the mind, it also closes the community by imposing controlling and monitoring measures. This causes a person, ultimately, to realize that the fear was justified since the control is legitimized by the attention paid to the possibility of an unrealized threat. This is a circular argument that is looking for affirmative elements to feed the mind. The fear of the unknown is also conserved in the shame of feeling irrational in a highly rational world.

The Sethian approach to the world and the mind consists of an attitude and a manner that constantly challenge the patterns and their right to exist. Through a systematic, exploratory, inquisitive, and sceptical attitude towards authority and truisms, the Sethian mind remains flexible. The method can best be described as a form of personality acrobatics, due to its focus on the ability to adjust to the transient nature of the world.

This necessary flexibility has several implications; among these is one's career and work situation. Sethians would thus probably prefer a business that has a great focus on development and self-management. This topic will not be discussed further, as it could have been a topic for a treatise of its own, but is mentioned for the benefit of the reader's own contemplation.

RELIGIOUS SETHIANISM

In the religious approach to this tradition, understanding the interaction between the psychological processes and the spiritual dimensions in man is essential.

The use of ceremonies and sacraments is also central to Sethianism and will be presented in the chapter on the methodological consequences of the Sethian narrative.

Every Sethian inquiry begins with Man, for by knowing Man, the Sethian will be able to trace the way back to the source and comprehend the content of the Mystery, and thus the nature of the Origin.

It is true that this may seem a strange approach to religion. It is a form of experimental religion, where the process is absolutely essential to understanding the aim properly. If the aim was given, it would not be possible to recognize it as the truth.

The goal is true by virtue of the journey to it. On this way the Sethians have designed ceremonies that act as beacons that can be followed like points of light on the horizon leading the way back to the spiritual home. In between these stationed lights, the initiate has to create light in his or her own material life. This might be done through interaction with others and through bringing forth one's own inner Man of light.

The religious Sethian is a spiritual wanderer who deliberately uses this wandering as a method; even though he might be situated at the same place throughout his whole life.

To understand religious Sethianism one must understand its psychological implications, together with its use of sacraments, as a vehicle for spiritual liberation.

Interpretational
consequences

"Fire, the flaming hell of liquid metal and liquid minerals below
us; and the deadly cold, empty, dead space [...] above us:
in other words: our life on this infinitely beautiful, lush and
green, moist paradisaical garden on a thin, thin crust of
temperate soil,
the succulent bliss of fertility and yield, that we live on."
[...]
"Is this mathematical, pedantic, microcosmic watchmaker's
workshop of timetables and necessity, all this terrible accuracy
in the dead cold space
-is it the lunatic asylum that it must be, if it has no meaning?
This ridiculous, absurd and, above all, totally senseless,
incredibly enormous universe; if it is without meaning,
it should cease to exist."
Powderhouse **by Jens Bjørneboe**

It is up to the individual to draw consequences and knowledge
from the Sethian myths and stories. The more we explore
mankind, creation, and the Mystery, the better the Sethian
tradition may serve as a key to escape one's personal, mental
prison.

The content of this chapter reflects some thoughts and ideas
of Masters and Initiates of the tradition, harvested from their
personal work with the stories.

The World

The world is, according to the Sethian tradition, the lowest level of material condensation. It is composed of the four elements; fire, air, water and earth, which combine, separate, and blend to form different compounds which make up everything in this world. The elements have, as does the rest of the creation of the demiurge, inner tensions and contradictions, such as fire against water and air against earth.

The Sethian is primarily concerned with the spiritual and psychological aspects of the elements, which may be considered as follows: Fire as energy, anger and lust; Water as emotions and melancholy; Air as the mental thoughts we shape our world with, but also obsessions and inconsistencies; and Earth as the mixture of all the others, or frugality, rigidity and persistence.

The world is also home to spiritual beings who affect humans in various ways. A group of these are Nebroel's demons, who benefit from this place, since it is a buffer zone, or a no-man's land, between the unbridled chaos and Yaldabout's so-called order.

The demons can be helpful to people seeking earthly goals, as human material pursuits help them to keep the material dream intact. It is equally unwise to make deals with them as it is with Yaldabout's angels. These beings have their own agenda which is to keep people in their custody. Yaldabout and Nebroel created the world out of dreams and desires. Yaldabout manages it with spiritual and physical laws, which make sense in the same way events in a dream make sense to the dreamer.

Taking this into consideration, the world appears as tripartite; one part being the replicated world, as Yaldabout saw it in the waters, and which is the false fullness or heaven. This is Yaldabout's paradisaical garden.

Secondly, there is the darkness on the outskirts of the chaos in which Yaldabout created the world, and is the place to which Nebroel has been banished. This is the realm of the unconscious repressed fantasies, anxiety and forbidden dreams.

Finally, there is the material world, a dried manifestation of Yaldabout's creation, bordering on the right to Yaldabout's Heaven or paradise, and to the left to Nebroel's Hell, and constitutes thus a scar where the two opposites meet.

In between these extremities, or rather as a background for them, is the true world, the Pleroma. It has no centre and its circumference is everywhere yet nowhere, even in the light and darkness of the world.

Therefore, the world has in itself no meaning. One can decide to give meaning to activities one takes part in, yet this is sympathetic meaning, not meaning in and of itself. For example, most people place meaning in interpersonal relations, career, ideas, desires etc. but this meaning consists only of cultural factors and emotions. This is not to say that people, our experiences and lives are unimportant or meaningless, but it does mean that what is important, is important because we make it so.

It is important to add meaning to our worldly life, as the opposite might lead to depression, anxiety and mental disorders.

True meaning is only to be found in the understanding of what is hiding behind the concept of Gnosis.

Then everything will truly be meaningful.

Morality

The Rulers confuse humanity in body and mind through the use of desire, grief, fear, and other unbalanced emotions. These might further lead to feelings such as envy, vanity, anger, bitterness and subservience. It is these and an unreasonable cultivation of one's lower desires that pull attention away from fulfilment.

Sethian morality is derived by questioning what binds the individual to the world and what frees him. This means that people are welcome to build a successful worldly life, but that they should not be too strongly attached to it. While we build our lives, we have to make sure that we are not possessed by our creations. One must for instance let the past be past, and not lose oneself to it. One should not desire anything or anyone in the world to the extent that one is not willing to do without it or them.

This being said, the world is what the Sethian makes of it. It may become an interesting and entertaining place for those who are not broken by its ups and downs.

About sin or hindrance

According to Sethian teaching, humans are born free from any sin and find themselves thrown into an existential impromptu situation in the world. One cannot blame the created for the creation, as this would constitute an illogical error of deduction. In other words Sethians do not share the view on sin found in Pistic Christianity. The connotations of the term 'sin', are so rooted in guilt and negativity that Sethians rarely use it. Instead they talk about sin as obstacles that limit people from experiencing and recognizing the Mystery. Sin, from the Sethian angle, is desire that leads to temporal goals, rather than to the Mystery, or awareness and deepening one's understanding of it.

All humans experience everyday situations in which they must make choices, and it is not always possible to choose the option that gives the least possible spiritual friction. We will always need to compromise. The important thing is never to compromise in mind, so that one does not create habits that obscure one's Gnosis. An obstacle transforms truth and its consequences in accordance with one's lower needs, so that convenience comes before the unfolding of the true being of Man.

Neither body nor mind are sinful. Nebroel does not own your body, even though matter and the subconscious are her natural habitat, just as Yaldabout's natural habitat is the mind and especially the habits and conscience. Through free will and knowledge, it is up to each individual to decide the place for Yaldabout and Nebroel in their own being.

LIFE AFTER DEATH AND THE END OF THE WORLD

The most futile of religious speculations concerns the afterlife and the end of time. Various Gnostic circles differ greatly in their understanding of this, some do not even talk about it at all.

We will not elaborate on the topic already discussed above, as the Abode of the Wise, nor present perspectives of other Gnostic schools, but will instead speak of those specific to Sethianism.

Those who have knowledge about their true Origin, and have allowed this truth to permeate, will at the end of their life once again experience the inner unity of all things, the unity behind all veils and shadows. Tradition states that all people will have opportunity to reintegrate into the Pleroma. The Wise will move between the worlds and facilitate this process. The soul of the pneumatic will burn up when it leaves the spheres of the Rulers, and the Abode of the Wise, and will thus re-enter into the Fullness.

Some will find Gnosis in the course of a lifetime; others will experience reincarnation, in which one will rhythmically move between the world and Yaldabout's so-called Paradise.

It is this cyclical process that continues until the end of time. Individuals who are unwilling to be reintegrated will, at the end of time, be dissolved along with the angels and demons that do not return into the Fullness.

The psychics and the hylics will be delivered through Yaldabout's self-knowledge and redemption, when he is once again united with Nebroel in one fulfilled entity that will release the material, spiritual and mental world and all that is trapped within it.

The sons and daughters of Cain and Abel will come together at that time, and in association with their spiritual counterpart they will receive Gnosis and redemption.

The last to be delivered from their afflictions are those who have betrayed the Holy Spirit, who wittingly turned away from the Fullness and their Gnosis. Their voluntary return to the world and the chaos beyond will cause them to be delivered last, or to perish in the resolution of all form.

In this way one might say that Sethianism has a positive view on life after death and the end of the world, since all will receive their reward in the end. It is only a matter of time, pleasure and suffering, and how each of us get to that point. It also has important implications on how one decides to live life in the world.

An individual can choose to be content with living a regular life, letting the spirit sleep inside the mental prison, or seek the amazing experiences that follow from the infinite possibilities inherent in the full realization of Man.

Methodological consequences

The Sethian tradition is, in addition to being a philosophy of life and an attitude towards all beings and the world, also a sacramental tradition. The purpose of the sacraments is, as mentioned in the section on religious Sethianism, to initiate and deepen the individual's relationship to the Mystery.

The sacraments are not absolutely necessary to acquire Gnosis, nor to grasp the redemptive Mystery. There is a myriad of paths to redemption, probably as many as there are people who have reached it.

The sacraments are the tools of the Sethian school, to assist their initiates on their way to fulfilment.

The tradition will always be based on the individual and his life experience gathered thus far. It is the function of the Masters and Initiators to initiate an individual understanding through past experience, and the use of tradition, teachings and sacraments. In this regard, the method is similar to that found in many Western esoteric orders.

The four sacraments are: Baptism, the Lower and the Higher Ascension, and the Communion or Eucharist. Baptism and the Lower and Higher Ascension are progressive steps, whilst the Eucharist or Communion provides an overall picture of the whole process and stabilizes it.

This is illustrated in the following table. Notice that the Eucharist embraces the whole process:

4. The Higher Ascension.	Eucharist
3. The Baptism of the Five Seals (the fifth seal)	Eucharist
2. The Lower Ascension	Eucharist
1. The Baptism of the Five Seals (the first four seals)	Eucharist

THE BAPTISM OF THE FIVE SEALS

The Baptism of the Five Seals is a reconstruction of the human being through the opening of five seals within its soul. This assists in the liberation of the qualities in man, making it possible to understand and see beyond the creation of the demiurge, and experience the relationship with the Fullness.

The sacrament consists of five separate parts, each with its own characteristic baptism, which has similarities with the ceremony indicated in the last part of *The book of the Great Invisible Spirit*. The ceremony in this book also includes invocations, purifications, anointing, and the granting of seals and symbols.

THE ASCENSION

The Lower Ascension:
The process that began in Baptism continues in The Lower Ascension, so as to provide the initiate with the means to rise up through Yaldabout's heavens and to explore and learn about the composition and mechanisms of the world. In order to implement such an ascent, the master will lead the initiate on the first ascent, and show him the names and symbols that open the sealed vaults of Heaven.

After this, it is the initiate's responsibility to undertake future journeys of his own.

The Higher Ascension:
The Higher Ascension requires a comprehensive release of the Man of Light within the human being. The Sethian is instructed in how to step into the Pleroma, to be born again there, to

consummate the one Mystery, and thus becoming a living chalice for this Mystery on earth.

This ascent is led by a master, as the initiate focuses on discovering the seals to his own birth. The master reveals to him the keys to the creation and the life of the Aeons, and reveals Man's relationship to these. The initiate is also taught how to master parallel living, i.e. living both here and there, by uniting both within his being.

THE EUCHARIST

The Eucharist is celebrated as an imitation of Christ's last supper. It follows the request given to his descendants, "do this in remembrance of me".

The tradition of remembering is not to remember that they ate together, but the holy operation that Christ performed to show his initiates how they could ceremonially transform themselves and realizing the Christ within.

By eating a ceremonially prepared Man-of-Light-tablet (bread), according to tradition, the individual's mental structure is gradually changed, so that the redemption is being prepared. After the Mystery is consummated, this sacrament continues to cultivate and maintain the fulfilled Man.

The Eucharist is a sacrament made for the initiate to partake of on a regular basis, and is thus for most Sethians, the cornerstone of their ceremonial practice.

Sethianism has a special communion ritual, but may if it is more convenient, share communion with other local Gnostic organizations.

DREAMWORKING

Next to the sacraments, dreamwork is the most important tool in unfolding the significance of the Mystery, for the way to widening one's knowledge implies opening the gates to the subconscious. Dreaming may either be part of regular sleep periods, or consist of waking dreams self-induced by the skilled initiate.

In the reception of the sacraments, the Sethian receives symbols to be used to open the sealed doors of the subconscious mind. The challenge of dreamwork is to determine which symbol belongs to which door, and to establish what constitutes a door in the chaotic and unchartered waters of the subconscious mind. Dreamwork is also a medium for exploring the Aeons through releasing the spirit and travelling through the spheres as the Man of Light.

This work is done by those who have understood the meaning of the Mystery, and have begun to actualize its implications.

SETHIANISM AND CEREMONIAL MAGIC

Sethianism also uses other methods and practices to reach the state of redemption. One of the best known of these is what is frequently referred to as ceremonial magic.

Magic can simply be defined as making changes according to the will. This means that all truly willed actions are magical acts, but it is in particular the metaphysical acts of will that are to be described here.

The magical practice especially used among Sethians is theurgy, which is Greek for God-work. Theurgy may consist of a wealth of methods, which have in common that their intentions are to make man divine.

Particularly well known methods are rituals to balance or offset the zodiacal and planetary influences upon human life, that is, to break free from Fate.

Sethians view the world as a complex and solid dream, which may be compared to an intelligent computer programme.

Magical rites are thus small programmes (or computer viruses), which are launched within the mainframe and thus change parts of it. It may be argued that the ceremonial practice of the Sethians can be compared to hackers invading a computer system.

The Method of Apatheia

> Become passers-by.
> *The Gospel of Thomas*

To live in the world without being possessed by the world, one cannot desire to really own anything, and must have some kind of detachment, which in Sethianism is called *Apatheia*.

The result of this might sound as if the Sethian road is one of renunciation, but this is not the case. You can own as much as you want, and be involved in numerous relationships, but must not cling to anything or anyone. This tradition is aptly expressed by the words, 'The Lord giveth and the Lord taketh away, blessed be the name of the Lord'.

In this world we cannot be sure of anything. We do not know how long we, or our loved ones, will live. We do not know if our health will last or about the future of our material welfare.

This means that the rule of thumb for all dealings with the world is that one cannot have any trust in the world or in its relations or its content; everything is changing, everything except the Mystery.

If you are unsure whether you are too dependent on something, you should try to live without it for a while, or even get rid of it. It might be an interesting experiment to smash an object that has great sentimental value, to know what feelings this generates.

If you live by this rule of thumb and avoid placing trust in the world it will change your attitude fundamentally, without making it a pathological excuse to avoid good and deep relationships with people. It may also give the serenity which is necessary to cultivate the redemption process.

This attitude can also lead to much joy connected to great and small events in life, and to a greater extent relate you to the present, instead of only reliving the past, lost in pleasant memories, or look forward to a future that has not, and maybe will not, take place.

So therefore: Carpe diem!

Institutional consequences

There is, at the time of writing, to the best of the author's knowledge, only one known Sethian school which does not mix Sethianism with other mystery traditions. This is *Sodalitas Sanctum Seth* (SSS), and the cover illustration on this book borrows the school's official seal.

The seal of the Sodalitas Sanctum Seth.

The Sacraments may be communicated within and outside the framework of an organization, but will in all cases require a Master. For those who want to know more about the SSS, there are, in the Appendix, excerpts of an interview with a Master from the SSS.

POSTSCRIPT

After having read the Sethian myth in this book, or similar stories in other books, one might be left with the question of whether there actually exist any spiritual or psychological variables, such as Yaldabout and Nebroel, trying to prevent us from knowing the true God, or our true self.

To this I can only reply that I do not know if they exist or not. But anyhow, whether they have an objective nature or are part of our minds, the mind and the world act as if they are realities on several levels.

Sethianism was probably founded on observations of the structures in human behaviour. Seeing our way of thinking and perceiving life, seeing the meaninglessness and unscrupulousness of nature; they asked this question:

Why is there so much suffering and despair in the world, and why are we here? The most obvious and rational religious answer would be: The world was not created by a good almighty God, and mankind is not really at home here.

Thus we can imagine the origin of Gnostic thinking, which after these first hypotheses turns to a quest for the true and benevolent God, and mankind's true home.

Sethianism is, as it is described here, a 'religion' for the rational, exploratory, pragmatic individual who wishes to seek God and truth through a different approach to religious life.

APPENDIX

MANIFESTO OF THE RESTORATION GNOSTICS

This Restoration is a restoration of the ancient Gnostic schools. We recognize that they all have the same core but have preferred different aesthetic expressions of the truth. This means that all schools, churches and orders that provide the Gnosis are equal. Discussions between the various groups are thus only questions regarding the optimal form and practice.

Restoration Gnostics are concerned with the language of the Gnostic traditions. Many years of Pistisistic use of many common concepts in the Jewish and Christian traditions have set an indelible colour on important terminology. Since language creates reality, it is important to re-establish the flexibility of the concepts by explicitly reinterpreting them.

Gnosis is further conveyed in many organizations that had their origin in the period before the First World War. It is therefore suitable for Restoration Gnostics to seek these expressions in their older structures for inspiration and further development of the tradition.

The form of the Gnostic story will always be told in ways that do not alienate modern man from its core. This means that different media and adaptation through storytelling is important to secure a future audience.

In working with Restoration Gnosticism the personal experience with the Mystery is of primary importance. This experience has emerged out of the source of the tradition, and is now the living expression of Gnosticism, the old source material being thus of secondary importance.

A good understanding of the content and implied meanings of the source texts is required so as to be able to be free from their limitations. This requires that Restoration Gnostics also hold a good academic understanding of source material, so they know what may be changed without dissolving the individuality of the particular tradition.

Restoration Gnostics must be able to create their own Gnostic writings, based on their own acquaintance with the Mystery.

Restoration Gnostics are educators and pragmatic artists. Traditions are regarded as didactic tools and artistic expressions in unfolding the ways of the Mystery.

The truth, which is described as the Mystery, is constant. Its expression is flexible and dependant on the era and the culture in which it is revealed.

THE ROAD TO GNOSIS

This is a short excerpt from an unpublished interview with an initiate of the SSS. It is included here to provide some perspectives on how a person was introduced to Gnosticism, and to give insight into some of the thoughts generated by this meeting, and how the meeting came to be.

Can you tell me a bit about how you began your religious quest?

When I was fifteen, I tried to find my place in the faith-based church. I had a good friend as a discussion partner, and together we explored the stories of the Bible, and often we came to the same paradox: One can only choose one of the following statements, given that God created the world and all people in it:
God is good
or
God is almighty.
His answer was most often, God is good, and he works in mysterious ways, therefore, he could ignore the *or*, and just add the quality of omnipotence.
This was an argument that I could never accept.
For me, the argument must either be God is good, but Satan is an adversary who is just as powerful as, or even more powerful than God. But I did not feel this to be right either.
The other option was more likely, and far more disturbing, namely that God is omnipotent, but not purely good. This bothered me, as a sincere seeker. Quite often this suspicion was present in the back of my head, a suspicion to which I would rather not seek the answer.
I guess I was afraid that I already knew the answer.

Was it in this context, that you became familiar with the Gnostic stories?

No, it was not until two years later that I heard about Gnosticism for the first time. This was when I came across a book that briefly described that there were many Christian gospels in early Christianity, but that only some of them were selected to be part of the New Testament.

This led me to read a detailed description of the myth communicated in *The Secret Book of John,* which presents the Gnostic mythology.

The result caused a deep disgust, mixed with a deep attraction and a strange feeling of receiving confirmation of something I had always known.

The tremendous dissonance this created between my slightly sceptical Christian faith and a story that explained everything that had bothered me was unnerving, and I didn't continue this contemplation until two years later, when I once again was haunted by this story.

I was then reconciled with the idea, and ready to go into what I had understood to be the redemptive way that can give peace to Faustian people, who cannot rest until all the mysteries are revealed and all secrets disclosed.

How would you describe the Gnostic way to an outsider?

Gnosticism is a group of traditions for those who cannot content themselves with mere faith, but still want to relate to a Christian frame of reference. It is a religion for those who, along with Alice in Wonderland, want to follow the white rabbit to the end of the road to see and experience what's there.

I like to think of it as a form of Experimental Theology, a name that is used in the SSS. The myth is told in many ways, but the common ground is that by understanding our human being, and its correct inner relations with God and nature, we are liberated, while still in the flesh.

Interview with a SSS-Teacher

This is an excerpt from the interview:

You describe Sodalitas Sanctum Seth as a school of Mysteries, but what separates this from other denominations?

SSS is not a church or a religion as such, but a sodality that is based on our experience of the Mystery or the Gnosis. We use the Sethian story as focus in interpreting and understanding this Mystery.
We are, in other words, building our teachings on the foundation of the old Sethian stories, and bringing them to light for new generations, whilst always honouring the unique expression of the Mystery in our tradition.
We perceive the SSS as a Gnostic Restoration tradition.

What does that mean?

Restoration Gnostics put the Mystery at the centre of their teachings, and work artistically in relation to ways of conveying this tradition in a modern or postmodern world, without breaking with the particular aesthetic expression of the tradition, or being limited by it.

How is SSS organized?

The teaching method of this school is built upon the relationship between a master and a student. The latter is an apprentice until he or she is ready to become an independent carrier of the tradition, and may even also become a master, and thus dedicate him or herself to passing on the tradition.

SSS as an organization does, in other words, consist of a spiritual lineage of teachers that we call masters.

The organization is led by a master. This particular master has as his function to ensure that the tradition survives throughout history. He protects the book *Charaxio*, which is the holy book of this school, and is a secret keeper of the Sethian plan.

A fully initiated master can freely create an SSS-community of masters and students, or work on their own.

In order to be part of the SSS, you must be affiliated with a master, and get training from him or her, and thus receive the sacraments. Masters in the SSS today do usually require that students take part in an esoteric order, which makes up the second part of the student's education and provides a multilateral approach to the work.

What orders are in question, and why is this necessary?

It is not necessary to be in any order, but we recommend it because it can provide other experiences and perspectives that strengthen the work. Orders are also social communities with opportunities to discuss views with others with similar interests and experiences. This will also help to loosen the bond between master and pupil, so that the student does not get trapped in a closed dependent relationship with a master.

There are two orders that are recommended on the basis of their resonance with the SSS [cf. "The Manifesto of the Restoration Gnostics ", presented in the appendix]. These are the *Sodalitas Rosae Crucis* and the *Ordre Reaux Croix*. These orders give the student a broad perspective, and a more versatile understanding of, respectively, magical and mystical approaches to the Mystery.

How does SSS recruit new members?

We do not. SSS has no e-mail address, so you have to be invited, or get in touch by intermediaries, as the SSS does not actively recruit new members. One possibility is to contact one of the two orders I mentioned earlier, as there are members of these Orders that also are students and masters of the SSS.

References and Recommended
FURTHER READING

Today, there is a wealth of books and texts that use the terms *Gnosis* and *Gnosticism*, without necessarily basing this on the tradition that gave rise to this category.

To help readers who wish to immerse themselves in the Gnostic tradition, I have made a list containing some books, which may provide enhanced understanding of Gnosticism, Sethianism and the mystery behind these traditions.

Pagels, Elaine: *The Gnostic Gospels*
This is a good introduction to Gnostic history and thought, and has become a classic.

King, Karen: *The Secret Revelation of John*
The best scholarly interpretation of the book referred to as the Gnostic Bible.

King, Karen: *The Gospel of Mary of Magdala. Jesus and the First Woman Apostle*
A good description of the Gnostic teachings. Mary Magdalene was one of, and maybe the most important of, the disciples of Jesus in the Gnostic tradition.

Amundsen, Christan: *Illumination: A Gnostic Handbook for the Post Modern World*
A good introduction to Gnosticism generally, written from a partaking point of view.

Mayer, Marvin: *The Nag Hammadi Scriptures*
The standard work on Gnosticism. The book consists of new translations of the most important Gnostic texts.

Angelus Silesius: *The Cherubinic Wanderer*
This is not a Gnostic work, but deals with the same Gnostic mystery in a great and poetic way.

Recommended Movies

The Matrix (1999)
The first *Matrix* film describes the protagonist's path to knowledge, which psychologically is quite similar to that found in Sethianism.

The Truman Show (1998)
This film shows the relationship between man and Yaldabout in a good and humorous way.

The thirteenth floor (1999)
The film treats the issue of the strength and credibility of our reality, and contains issues regarding Metanoia.

Gabriel (2007)
Gabriel explores the problem of being placed in a world that does not fit with one's nature.

Equilibrium (2002)
A future-dystopia, which deals with the question of whether humans can be modified to fit into the world.

Vanilla Sky (2001)
A good film about dream and reality.

The Cube (1997)
A film about meaningless structures and their impact on the human mind.

Donnie Darko (2001)
A good film about the fragility of reality.

Alice in Wonderland (1951)
A classical movie about meaning and meaninglessness.

The Order (2003)
This film joins the debate over religious institutions' monopoly on salvation and redemption.

Blade runner (1982)
Blade runner is a classical AI film. It debates issues surrounding the relationship between the creator and the created.

The Bothersome Man (2006)
A fantastic Norwegian film about meaning, meaninglessness and existential experience of captivity.

www.ingramcontent.com/pod-product-compliance
Lightning Source LLC
Chambersburg PA
CBHW030400100426
42812CB00028B/2779/J

*9 7 8 8 2 9 9 8 2 4 3 7 8 *